The joy of the series, of reading *Remote Control, Golf Ball, Driver's License, Drone, Silence, Glass, Refrigerator, Hotel*, and *Waste* . . . in quick succession, lies in encountering the various turns through which each of their authors has been put by his or her object . . . The object predominates, sits squarely center stage, directs the action. The object decides the genre, the chronology, and the limits of the study. Accordingly, the author has to take her cue from the *thing* she chose or that chose her. The result is a wonderfully uneven series of books, each one a *thing* unto itself."

Julian Yates, *Los Angeles Review of Books*

The Object Lessons series has a beautifully simple premise. Each book or essay centers on a specific object. This can be mundane or unexpected, humorous or politically timely. Whatever the subject, these descriptions reveal the rich worlds hidden under the surface of things."

Christine Ro, *Book Riot*

. . . a sensibility somewhere between Roland Barthes and Wes Anderson."

Simon Reynolds, author of *Retromania: Pop Culture's Addiction to Its Own Past*

OBJECTLESSONS

A book series about the hidden lives of ordinary things.

Series Editors:

Ian Bogost and Christopher Schaberg

In association with

BOOKS IN THE SERIES

grave

ALLISON C. MEIER

BLOOMSBURY ACADEMIC
NEW YORK · LONDON · OXFORD · NEW DELHI · SYDNEY

BLOOMSBURY ACADEMIC
Bloomsbury Publishing Inc
1385 Broadway, New York, NY 10018, USA
50 Bedford Square, London, WC1B 3DP, UK
29 Earlsfort Terrace, Dublin 2, Ireland

BLOOMSBURY, BLOOMSBURY ACADEMIC and the Diana logo are trademarks of
Bloomsbury Publishing Plc

First published in the United States of America 2023

Cover design: Alice Marwick

Bloomsbury Publishing Inc does not have any control over, or responsibility for, any third-
party websites referred to or in this book. All internet addresses given in this book were
correct at the time of going to press. The author and publisher regret any inconvenience
caused if addresses have changed or sites have ceased to exist, but can accept no
responsibility for any such changes.

Whilst every effort has been made to locate copyright holders the publishers would be
grateful to hear from any person(s) not here acknowledged.

Library of Congress Cataloging-in-Publication Data

Names: Meier, Allison C. (Allison Christine), 1985- author.
Title: Grave / Allison C. Meier.
Description: New York : Bloomsbury Academic, 2023. | Series: Object lessons | Includes
bibliographical references and index. | Summary: "Examines the design of the grave and
how the ways in which we care for the dead are changing as old systems of burial are
seen as expensive and unsustainable while new trends are emerging for people who
want a more personal, meaningful final statement"–Provided by publisher.
Identifiers: LCCN 2022028626 (print) | LCCN 2022028627 (ebook) | ISBN 9781501383656
(paperback) | ISBN 9781501383663 (epub) | ISBN 9781501383670 (pdf) | ISBN
9781501383687 (ebook other)
Subjects: LCSH: Burial. | Cemeteries. | Cremation. | Dead.
Classification: LCC GT3190 .M45 2023 (print) | LCC GT3190 (ebook) |
DDC 393/.1–dc23/eng/20220804
LC record available at https://lccn.loc.gov/2022028626
LC ebook record available at https://lccn.loc.gov/2022028627

ISBN: PB: 978-1-5013-8365-6
ePDF: 978-1-5013-8367-0
eBook: 978-1-5013-8366-3

Series: Object Lessons

Typeset by Deanta Global Publishing Services, Chennai, India
Printed and bound in the United States of America

To find out more about our authors and books visit www.bloomsbury.com
and sign up for our newsletters.

CONTENTS

1 THE GRAVE

OUR HOUSE OF ETERNITY

At one point in writing this book, I was told about New York City, my home: "It's the last place I'd want to die." Even as someone who regularly walks among the tombstones as a cemetery tour guide, I had never considered if I lived in a good place to die. Yet as I looked around at the options, they were limited, as they are for most Americans, to a casket burial inside a concrete vault or cremation.

The grave is the period to a sentence I am still writing. Some of us get whole paragraphs and this last punctuation mark is not as crucial, but for others, it is a vital statement to show that they were here. Although we all die, the grave is a choice. It may not be our choice; it may be decided by friends, family members, or strangers if we die alone or unclaimed. It may be a final declaration of everything we believed or a reflection of who we were in life, whether wealthy or poor, or part of a family, society, or faith. It may be an act of necessity amid catastrophes and wars. It may be a form of concealment; it may be purposefully forgotten underneath layers of a city.

Death is the ultimate great leveler that no one has yet to cheat despite ongoing attempts, from the Emperor Qin Shi Huang's poisonous quest for a "drug of deathlessness" (which didn't stop him from being buried over 2,000 years ago in China with an army of Terracotta Warriors), to the current Silicon Valley ventures to arrest aging and death itself through growing new organs and artificial intelligence. Those who devote the most energy to evading the grave usually have the least to lose in its obliteration of self as wealth and power wane slowly.

When I think of the grave, I do not dwell on death. I am more curious about how it is designed to mean something to those left behind, and how our relationship to it and its visibility in the United States as a place of private grief expressed in public have shifted over time. Overwhelmingly, our graves are not as diverse as our dead, and what seems traditional is relatively new. The old churchyards with their ghoulish skulls carved in brownstone and slate once called on passersby to cast an eye and remember their fate. In a move to the outskirts that predated the suburbs are the 19th-century cemeteries, frequently absorbed by sprawl yet still testifying to a belief in the edifying power of a landscape that could mourn as well as extoll a proper life through the examples of those who were here before. The uniform lawn-style cemeteries that dominated the 20th century with grass trimmed to golf course precision and orderly rows of granite monuments, where so many of us have interred our families, were shaped by the commodification and homogenization of the grave.

The grave started simply but was done with care. Some of the oldest known modern human burials include the Qafzeh Cave in Israel where individuals from the Middle Paleolithic period appear intentionally interred together, with chunks of ochre found near their bones.[1] In Kenya, a child who died 80,000 years ago was discovered in a cave, their legs carefully tucked to their chest and their head on a pillow, a gesture not dissimilar from today's corpses arranged in silk-lined caskets.[2]

Even as the grave's rituals and shape have changed, it endures as something that makes us human. Unlike the universal emotion of grief, however, the grave is cultural and informed by beliefs, such as whether the corpse is an empty vessel to be discarded or to be attended to with love, and if death is the end or a transition. French anthropologist Robert Hertz was one of the earliest scholars of death's cultural significance. He wrote in 1907 that the "body of the deceased is not regarded like the carcass of some animal: specific care must be given to it and a correct burial; not merely for reasons of hygiene but out of moral obligation."[3] He researched the burial practices of the Pacific region—particularly the Dayak people of Borneo—but his observations on this time of transformation, when a person becomes a corpse, can be applied across the world. (Hertz died in 1915 at 33 while fighting for France in World War I. I could not find his grave in my research, nor if he has one.)

What a grave looks like, where it is located, how it is marked, and how long it is expected to endure have been evolving for as long as people have been dying, which is to say, a very long time. The cultural process of dying has influenced these changes, such as the desire to die at home instead of at a hospital now leading to more home funerals and green burials. So has the faith (or not) in an afterlife or some existence beyond the veil. As 19th-century French architect Eugène Viollet-le-Duc observed, "Civilizations, at all levels of the scale, have manifested the nature of their beliefs in another life by the way they have treated the dead."[4]

A grave has been as extravagant as a pyramid that stands for millennia or as minimal as an unmarked body in the earth allowed to decompose into obscurity. It often perpetuates the divisions of life, showing who was worthy of veneration and who was deemed deserving of only the simplest of memorials. It is as permanent as a granite mausoleum the size of a small house and as mobile as an urn. It is as unsentimental to the corpse as Tibetan sky burial, where the deceased is offered to the vultures, and as far from interment in the ground as a coffin suspended from a cliff in the ancient funerary practices of central China. It has been a satellite hurtling through space embedded with ashes and an artificial reef made with cremated remains at the bottom of the ocean. It is one last chance to say this is what I believed, this is the family I was a member of, this is the community I lived in. It remembers that someone was here, whether for a hundred years or just a few hours.

A grave is a final act of care, like the congregation of the Chapel of the Cross in Madison, Mississippi, which comes together to dig graves for each other by hand, or the father who in 1865 in New York built a tomb with a window for his departed eight-year-old boy who was afraid of the dark.[5]

A grave remembers what the living loved. An Ohio man's family buried him in 2014 inside a Plexiglas box astride his favorite 1967 Harley-Davidson motorcycle. The ashes of film critic Archer Winsten were scattered at his headstone by the ski lift of Hunter Mountain in the Catskills in 1997, paying tribute to his passion for these slopes.[6,7]

A grave is a journey, sometimes around the world, as bodies travel in airplane cargo to be repatriated to the earth of where the departed considered home. The United Kingdom has traces of the medieval "corpse roads" where bodies were carried, sometimes over miles, to a churchyard.[8]

A grave is a destination. Elvis's grave at Graceland in Memphis, Tennessee, still draws an annual candlelight vigil on the anniversary of his death. Magicians leave cards and broken wands on Houdini's grave in Machpelah Cemetery in Queens, New York, and for years convened there on Halloween, his death day, to see if he would escape these mortal chains.

A grave recalls what was here before. The 19th-century headstones of Richard and Catherine Dotson are in the runway at Savannah/Hilton Head International Airport in Georgia.

Their family preferred they remain undisturbed when their graveyard became a tarmac.[9] A Franklin, Indiana, traffic median contains the 1831 grave of Nancy Kerlin Barnett. When the road was planned in 1905, her relatives refused to relocate their ancestor, so the cars had to go around.[10]

A grave forgets. Across the United States there are cemeteries for patients who died in mental institutions and were buried under numbers instead of names. A cemetery I visited near one of these asylums—Letchworth Village in Rockland County, New York—was used between 1917 and 1967.[11] It is dotted with T-shaped metal stakes marked with numbers, forcing a final anonymity in death.

A grave is a tool of oppression and control in genocides and dictatorships. Some are denied a burial, buried anonymously in a mass grave, or their families are given no knowledge of what became of them.

A grave turns the dead into symbols. In 1921, a soldier's unidentified remains were placed in a large marble tomb at Arlington National Cemetery to remember all the unknown dead in war. The regimented tombstones that process over the surrounding grass—only distinguished by names, dates, and selected religious or secular symbols—echo a message of selfless sacrifice. Across the globe are these American military cemeteries that appear nearly the same no matter their time or distance, the rhythm of names and dates feeling like an endless war.

A grave upholds and bridges divides. On the other side of a wall from the rest of the cemetery at Fort Reno, Oklahoma,

I found the gravestones for German and Italian prisoners of war who were among the thousands brought to the state during World War II.[12] Over another wall in Roermond in the Netherlands, two stone hands clasp, connecting the graves of a Catholic woman and her Protestant husband who died in 1880. They refused to be separated by the religious divisions of the cemetery.[13]

A grave is a punishment, a final derision to the executed criminal denied a tombstone or a plot. In Florence, Alabama, a historical marker states that the murderous outlaw "Mountain" Tom Clark was in 1872 lynched by a mob and then buried in the road, an affront to his brag that "no one would ever run over Tom Clark."[14] When suicide was a crime in England, a body was sometimes stabbed with a stake and buried at a crossroads, a practice only ended by an 1823 Act of Parliament.[15]

A grave prepares for the inevitable, whether buying a plot or setting aside money for your last rites. In the early 1900s, Sears, Roebuck and Company sold mail-order granite monuments, and traveling salesmen peddled caskets and customizable tombstones to cash in on the new American funerary business. This foresight can backfire. As the 20th century was nearing its end, hundreds of thousands of people who had pre-carved their headstones with a date beginning "19" had to pay for an update.[16] With extended life expectancies comes the delay of death's best-laid plans.

A grave is rarely just a place to dispose of the dead. Death is random and chaotic, but the grave imposes order, conveys social values, and provides catharsis and connection. We will all have a grave someday, shaped by how we lived and died, what we valued, and who was there to care for us at the end.

I have led cemetery tours in New York City since 2011, but for much of my life, the grave stayed, as it does for many Americans, at the periphery of my experiences with death. My family dies like any other, but there were no traditions of decorating a relative's grave on holidays or pilgrimages to ancestral burial grounds. Aside from the occasional funeral, the grave was invisible.

The grave was not always so easy to overlook. When the care of the dead changed in the 19th century with practices like embalming and cremation that required special equipment and facilities, the grave professionalized. As childhood mortality has declined, and medical advances have extended life, we have also dealt less and less with sudden and constant death. It is distant and controlled, often happening out of view in hospitals, hospices, or nursing homes. Morgues and funeral homes handle the corpse; the cemetery staff excavates the ground before the body arrives in the hearse. It is very easy not to think about the grave.

That does not mean there are no thriving practices with closer connections to the grave. Chinese and Chinese Americans celebrate the Qingming grave tending festival throughout the country in spring. In Terlingua, Texas, a stone's throw from the Mexican border, I stopped in the cemetery on a November day following Día de los Muertos. Each grave had at least one candle, even those without names that likely had become unknowns from long ago mining days. Some were covered with candles and gifts; others were full of beer and liquor bottles left by revelers who honored the departed at their resting place. These celebrations bring the grave to life—an exception in a country where it is typically characterized by austerity and distance from daily life.

My family, like that of many Americans, has moved far from where our relatives set down their last roots. Some family graves I have visited only virtually, such as my great grandmother's brother's 1897 grave in Clairemont, Texas, a place which is now a ghost town. On the online crowdsourced compendium FindaGrave.com, I can see photos from 2011 and 2015 taken by strangers of his headstone made from cast zinc that gives it a bluish tint and makes it look brand new. I can glimpse the reddish earth in the background. A little lamb above his name indicates immediately, before I read his age of "2 years and 12 days," that he died young. Graves balance two distinct tasks of remembering a person while capturing cultural meaning so that we can understand them in an instant. I may never visit this place, nor may any of my extended living family, yet here is this small monument to a child that has stood for over a hundred years with no one left to mourn.

Only when my grandmother on my father's side—my last grandparent to go—had her funeral did I spend time looking at the Meier family plot, full of names I knew and many I did not. It's in a bucolic cemetery on the edge of what was once the German part of St. Louis, Missouri. My ancestors are gathered there under modest stones, with names that echo their recent immigration, like Otto and August. They left these names in granite to be remembered by their family—me—but there I was, decades later, unable to remember who they were aside from some brief biographical facts. I took some white roses from the heap on my grandma's metal casket, an object that felt as huge as the car she drove well into old age, and put one on each marker. There is no room left in this plot, so my name will never join them.

We did not see my grandmother's casket lowered into the ground alongside my grandfather, her final wishes fulfilled, or the dirt filled in the grave. Like most of the physical tasks around death, interment is now out of family hands. Our family's role, instead, was to attend a brief graveside ritual and then move on before the grave itself was filled.

I became a cemetery tour guide by chance. When I moved to New York City from my home state, Oklahoma, in 2009, I was unmoored in my career and words. What could I say in a city so big that had not already been said? I happened to rent an apartment in the sliver of a neighborhood wedged between Brooklyn's Green-Wood Cemetery and the New York Harbor. I had never seen a cemetery like Green-Wood, with its soaring Gothic entrance arch that resembles the front of a cathedral and, as an extra uncanny twist, is crowned with a nest built by a squawking colony of non-native green monk parrots. Inside are paths that wind through thousands of monuments, ranging from looming obelisks to delicately carved marble statues. It is a place where the past feels tangible and the stories are limitless. As the late cultural geographer Terry G. Jordan observed, "we are closer to our forefathers when treading upon the ground where they lie buried."[17] In Green-Wood, I could see over a century of people spread over the rolling hills, their tombstones speaking to who they had been. All I had to do was listen.

A couple of years after my first visit, I began leading tours as I saw an opportunity to tell stories that others were not. The graves of military heroes and business tycoons populate most historic cemetery maps, but I wanted to know more about the people not immortalized with names on streets, companies, or endowments, whose final physical trace on the city might be their grave. An early tour I created was on disasters of New York. I tracked down victims of events that have no memorial in the city, like the September 16, 1920, Wall Street bombing that killed 40, and the November 1, 1918, Malbone Street wreck where over 90 people died in a train derailment in Brooklyn, making it New York's deadliest subway crash.[18] I have run my hand over the shrapnel scars that pock the limestone of 23 Wall Street and paused to read the marker at my neighborhood subway stop that remembers the dead of Malbone Street—an event so awful the thoroughfare was renamed Empire Boulevard—but there is little else to memorialize events that those who experienced them likely thought could never be forgotten.

I have looked for those buried in unmarked plots where the grass grows long—from acclaimed artists who died suddenly to vaudeville magicians whose stars had faded. There are the women who died in childbirth solely marked as "wife," memorialized with marble carvings of angels spiriting them away or cradling their stillborn children. There are carved oak leaves and acorns on tombstones to represent longevity, sometimes with an acorn depicted as missing so that the viewer knows a legacy has continued. Clasped hands adorn monuments of couples and siblings, one hand appearing to let go or perhaps greet the other in some afterlife, their bond unbroken by the impenetrable veil that has fallen between them. I wanted to learn something about the person mourned who lived in this city before me, even if their name has long ago vanished in the weathering of the marble.

Over the years, I have led walks at Green-Wood and other cemeteries, including Woodlawn Cemetery in the Bronx, with its elaborate Gilded Age mausoleums, and Hartsdale Pet Cemetery in Hartsdale, New York, where cats, dogs, guinea pigs, lizards, and other cherished creatures are buried. In the busy streets of Manhattan, I have shared how a block looked a century or more ago when it was a graveyard and what bones are probably resting beneath a park or intersection.

All of this has caused me to view the grave differently and examine how it has succeeded and failed. And realizing how much of this dense city is taken over by the dead has made me consider that while graves are valuable portals of history, they often do not serve the living. There must be changes to make them meaningful to the people who live here now.

I do not want a burial in a cemetery, nor the grim and impersonal funeral that generally precedes it. To be in a monotonous expanse of stones where the only thing differentiating my monument is my name and two dates feels like a waste, both in the cost and in the land it would occupy. And as none of my relatives had the finances or foresight to build a giant mausoleum where I could take my spot among the expired, my choices are few. In my living will documents I have asked to be cremated, but this is more out of convenience for the ones I'd leave behind rather than a genuine passion for being transformed into ash. Even my request about where to scatter my remains—I named a favorite state park in Oklahoma but anywhere with good trees will do—makes me worry that dumping a bunch of crushed bone fragments on a lovely environment is not the kindest way to go out.

Yet when I look at what's available, there is not much else. I live in the densest metropolitan area in the country. The cemeteries are crowded and pricey. A 2019 *New York Times* story reported that a New York City plot could cost between $4,500 and $19,000 (unless I wanted to get a bargain on Staten Island for under $3,000).[19] Former Mayor Edward I. Koch said he spent $20,000 so he could rest in Manhattan at Trinity Cemetery, where he was buried in 2013.[20] There are only four crematories for a population of over eight million, so even that can be inaccessible.[21] The closest place certified by the Green Burial Council is Sleepy Hollow Cemetery, about 30 miles north of the city, and it is just a small section of the cemetery.

I have written all of this book during the COVID-19 pandemic, which at its height revealed how vulnerable the city's funerary systems are to catastrophe, from crematories becoming backlogged to the refrigerated trucks set up for months on a pier in Brooklyn as a temporary morgue.[22] No, this is not a place I want to die. Yet it is unclear if this time of mass death will result in actual change.

To cover an entire history of the grave would be to chronicle all of human history, and that would be a very lengthy book indeed. Instead, I set out to look at the grave of the past, present, and future, as someone who has spent more time in cemeteries than most. This is an exploration of the American grave, how we got to where we are now, and how the ways we care for the dead are changing.

Cremation continues to gain in popularity, and more unconventional ideas have the potential to become part of our systems of death. They include human composting, where the dead become soil that's used to restore forests; water cremation, where the body falls apart in a more sustainable process than burning cremation; and green burial, where nothing but a shroud or plain coffin separates the body from the earth. More speculative ideas are on the horizon, like biomass that could illuminate bridges and transgenic trees containing the DNA of the departed. The grave may not and perhaps cannot look as it has in the past. Do we need spaces of ritual in an increasingly nomadic world where visiting our great-grandparents' tombs is uncommon, and collective memorial is as likely to happen online as around a casket? Could more options for the grave make the most unavoidable of fates a more dignified and communal experience for all? Or will the inequities that have long been a part of the grave persist?

2 NAVIGATING THROUGH NECROGEOGRAPHY

On a brutally hot July day, I climbed the stairs that crisscross to a platform on the top of a landform in Pinson Mounds State Archaeological Park south of Jackson, Tennessee. The 72-foot-tall Sauls Mound may seem an unremarkable hill until you consider human hands built it, hauling baskets of dirt—tens of thousands of cubic meters of it, all chosen with care and purpose—to this spot. For hundreds of years, it was a destination for people who traveled miles to mark solstices, equinoxes, and death. Surrounding it are about 15 surviving mounds that had burial and ceremonial uses in what is the country's largest known mound complex from the Middle Woodland period, with construction dating roughly between 100 and 350 CE.[1] Many of the earthworks are hard to see now, appearing as blips on the terrain. Some include cremated human remains; others have entire burials. The Twin Mounds, for instance, are conjoined burial mounds that stand over 20 feet. They were formed with varying layers of specifically selected earth, some likely brought from far away, to create a contrasting stratum of red, gray, white, and brown. In an earthwork effigy that appears like a giant bird of prey, just one person is buried, and although centuries have passed, and their name and identity are lost, we can discern from this grave the prestige it signified. Archaeologist Robert C. Mainfort Jr., in his extensive research on the Pinson Mounds, wrote that being interred here made someone "part of something greater than themselves and their social roles in life."[2]

No other visitors were around on that day, and only the slow circles of a small airplane cutting through the blue sky disrupted the quiet at the top of the mound. It is a rare place in this country where you can look at the topography of the past and see the role of mortuary activities in a site of ceremony, where each act of building reinforced the connections between life and death.

"I think that this place is still a sacred site, especially to Indigenous people, but also just to the regular person," Park Ranger Dedra Irwin told me. "Keeping these places protected gives us a story and a way to climb back in time to our ancestors and see what they were doing back then. If we didn't have this place protected with the state, there's no telling what we would have lost."

The Pinson Mounds are among several mounds sites in the Midwest and Southeast. While their activity predated European colonization, many mounds either eroded or were leveled when land was settled, farmed, and developed. The graves some contained were routinely obliterated, their artifacts churned up, destroyed, or stolen. It was common in the late 18th and early 19th centuries for white people to link the mounds to a lost civilization rather than the living Indigenous people, reinforcing that their land, past, and even remains were not their own.[3] The Native American Graves Protection and Repatriation Act (NAGPRA)—which requires that sites with remains "must at all times be treated with dignity and respect"—was only enacted in 1990.[4] For too many years, the idea of a grave as a place worthy of protection did not extend to Indigenous burial grounds, and the remains taken for museums, anthropology collections, and otherwise dispersed or destroyed are a legacy still widely unacknowledged.

It is impossible to examine the American grave without reckoning with the fact that the country is built on the colonization of Indigenous cultures that had their own deathways. Some graves have been revered as sacred—the tombs of presidents and the national military cemeteries—while others have been repeatedly treated as disposable. This hasn't just occurred with ancient mounds, but also in the removal of more recent burial grounds. In the Zion Episcopal Church cemetery in Queens, I visited a large boulder split in two, a tree growing through the center. An inscription reads: "Here rest the last of the Matinecoc," referring to the Matinecock people who lived in the New York City area and, despite the erroneous claim carved in stone, continue to have descendants here. What this actually marks are remains from an Indigenous burial ground that was removed when the city widened a street. An October 20, 1931, photograph in the NYC Municipal Archives shows workers with shovels carving a trench in the earth to remove these graves while curious onlookers stand by. James E. Waters, known as Chief Wild Pigeon, described in a 1919 letter how earlier burying grounds were desecrated, forcing the Matinecock to this spot "along the roadside where the iron shoes of the pale face horses instead of the soft moccasin tread, sleep the dead of the family and several whites too poor to own a grave."[5] As his 1927 obituary stated, he attempted for years in the courts to protect the graves, and while he could not save them, he was able to get the bodies moved to this plot at Zion Episcopal Church.[6]

There is some irony that, alongside the widespread relocation and desecration of Indigenous burial grounds, the American grave became permanent and forever.

It is something of an act of optimism to believe that this country of open land—ignoring the Indigenous people already on it—would never run out of room. The United States does very little reburial or reuse of plots. So when a body is buried, we expect it will be there alone in perpetuity. Yet across the globe, it is more common to have a plot as a renewable lease—most people's graves are located in community ossuaries and other mass burial spaces. In Germany, graves are up for renewal after 20 to 30 years; in China, a standard is 50 to 70 years.[7,8] At the Cimetière du Père-Lachaise in Paris, a space can be had for 10, 30, or 50 years, with the option to renew.[9] The City of London Cemetery & Crematorium has tackled its lack of space by reusing graves that are at least 75 years old.[10] Recycling graves isn't solely a matter of space; it's a way to sustain a cemetery. If plots can't be reused, a cemetery could go bankrupt and fall into disrepair, becoming a hazard to visitors with deteriorating monuments destabilized by overgrown foliage and erosion.

If the estimated 107 billion people who ever lived had a grave in perpetuity, their tombs would outnumber us at least 15 to one.[11] Even back in 1950, the American Society of Planning Officials warned that "we have already reached the point at which the distribution of land between the living and the dead is a serious problem."[12] There has been no uprising of the living against the dead yet, but particularly in urban areas, the demand for space given over to graves could heighten in the coming decades.

"The idea that we should each get an individual grave forever is clearly an American invention," said Tanya Marsh, a Professor of Law at Wake Forest University and a rare expert in cemetery law whose extensive scholarship includes a focus on disposition, or the final disposal of human remains. She told me she practiced commercial real estate law before arriving at Wake Forest and realized that this could be a subset of real estate law, but with its own complicated and very long-term rules. "It's just an endlessly fascinating area of the law that the vast majority of lawyers know nothing about," she said. "And of course, we're all going to die, and we're surrounded by cemeteries, and it is the most practical thing in the world to actually understand this. So, the lack of interest of others is equally fascinating to me."

To grasp how we got to the present—with a grave perpetually occupying space—we have to go back centuries. Marsh explained that the European colonists brought over their burial practices, including those of the Church of England, where members had a right to burial at the local parish where the Church then controlled the remains.

"Since the Church owned the consecrated ground and held the bodies in trust, it could basically do what it wanted to with them," Marsh said. "That meant a lot of grave recycling—burial in an unmarked grave until the body was reduced to a skeleton, and then the bones could be moved to a communal ossuary or charnel house to make room for more burials."

She added that the only way to avoid this eventual mass burial was to pay to be interred under the church building or commission a permanent marker. This was not something everyone could do. When places like Trinity Church in Manhattan were conducting burials, they continued this practice of grave recycling and added more burials on top of the older ones. It was only when settlement spread out of urban areas that grave recycling mostly ended in the United States. Although some places continued it—New Orleans's subtropical climate speeds decomposition and allows for a system of regularly turning over vaults while previous burials join a shared ossuary—the grave largely stopped being a place of impermanence.

"We had a lot of land and that land—outside of cities—was relatively cheap, and there was no reason we couldn't sell people a grave in perpetuity," Marsh said. "And we've been doing it so long that now that's just the way Americans think it has to be done."

From my home in Brooklyn, I can walk to four distinct kinds of American cemeteries. This navigation by necrogeography—or how a place has organized space for the dead—reveals how the grave changed in the time Marsh described.

The oldest is the late 18th century Dutch Reformed Church at the corner of Flatbush and Church avenues. It is among the city's oldest surviving structures, and bricks cut from the Manhattan schist in the bedrock give its façade a mottled color.[13] In its foundation are stones salvaged from the 17th-century church that preceded it, which dates to a 1654 mandate from Peter Stuyvesant, the last Dutch director-general of the colony of New Netherland.[14] A century after the 1664 English takeover of what is now New York City, it would not have been unusual to hear Dutch spoken at this intersection.[15]

The death practices of the Dutch Reformed Church were brought over and adapted from Europe. Early in its history, people were buried under the church; later, the churchyard was expanded, its now-archaic tombs worthy of a Hammer horror film. Indeed, H. P. Lovecraft, who lived for a time on nearby Parkside Avenue, described "its iron-railed yard of Netherlandish gravestones" in his tale of devil worship, "The Horror at Red Hook."[16] When the gate is unlocked, you can find headstones dating to 1759. Many have winged souls, the cherub-like faces carved with mournful expressions and bordered with wings, and the Dutch words *Hier leyt begraven*, "Here lies buried."

The churchyard is a quiet place that can feel forgotten along the busy commercial corridor of Flatbush. Over the 20th century, the neighborhood became a hub for immigration and is now known as Little Caribbean; the church now offers Spanish services and Ghanian worship. While its graves are highly visible through the fence, it's rare to see someone visiting them.

After the Dutch, English colonists likewise transported their traditions of the grave to the city. The oldest surviving headstone in Manhattan is in Trinity Churchyard, part of the island's first Anglican church. It is a grim two-sided marker for Richard Churcher, who died at five years old on August 5, 1681.[17] On one side are Churcher's name and date of death; on the other is a skull and crossbones and a winged hourglass so heavily carved they are strikingly visible even after over 300 years in the open air. In the early days of colonial settlement, there were few distinctions in the mourning of a young life from those privileged to grow old. The visceral imagery of life's decay on Churcher's tombstone echoes the surrounding monuments that remind the viewer again and again of the inevitability of death. A typical epitaph goes:

Behold and see as you pass by
As you are now so once was I
As I am now you soon shall be
Prepare for death & follow me.

The Puritans allowed a rare freedom on their headstones to express mortal warnings. They only practiced image-making in their graveyards, not in the churches. Even if a person was not literate, the carved hourglasses and winged death's heads would be reminders of the need to repent before the ghoulish visage that each human holds below the skin was revealed.

In an 1881 book on the history of the area by Gertrude Lefferts Vanderbilt, there is note of "a colored woman by the name of Flora" and two other "domestics" named Diana and Cato who were buried at the Dutch Reformed Church, although according to the New York City Cemetery Project there is no mention of them on a 1914 inventory.[18,19] Nothing today matches Vanderbilt's description of where they were interred, a place "separated by the high fence" from the rest of the burial ground. When the churchyard was active, most Black people were buried in a place long ignored.

While sites like the Dutch Reformed Church are landmarked and survive, the historic burial grounds where enslaved and free Black people cared for their dead were often built over and given little preservation attention. Slavery was a foundational part of New York City, from Dutch to British to American rule. The state did not abolish it until 1827, and in the heart of New York's Financial District—Wall Street—

there was a slave market. The segregation that persisted for decades after slavery also endured in death. On December 7, 1890, the *Brooklyn Daily Eagle* reported that "except in isolated instances, the color line is strictly drawn at the grave," adding that in many of the city's cemeteries, "the bodies of blacks may not be interred in the same section . . . with those of whites."[20]

Local activism has recently brought attention to the Flatbush African Burial Ground. It was at Bedford and Church avenues—just a block from the Dutch Reformed Church—and its former land has been vacant since a school was demolished in 2016. An 1855 map of the town of Flatbush shows that here was the "Negro Burial Ground."[21] Records of it are scarce, but there is a March 29, 1810, obituary in the *Long-Island Star* for an enslaved woman named Eve whose "remains were piously interred in the African burying ground of the village of Flatbush, attended by a great concourse of the people of colour."[22] Plans announced in October 2020 to build affordable housing at the site have been contentious, as many want to see it turned into a memorial and community space. A city announcement about the development noted that an archaeological excavation found "a small number of fragments of human remains, which may be associated with a historical burial ground for people of African ancestry."[23] By fall of 2021, the chain link fence around the lot where the grass had grown wild was an informal memorial. Flower planters made from cans and jars were affixed to the fence, and signage remembered Eve and another woman—Phyllis

Jacobs—whose burials were recorded. Large colorful letters spelled out: "African Burial Ground. Truth Is My Compass. What Is Left?" No one walking by could miss what was once so easy to overlook: that this was where a community mourned its dead, and the graves had not been honored.

Since colonization, the white and wealthy have been able to secure their remains while others frequently have not. Even the design of the grave has been dictated by those in power. In 1971, Ann and Dickran Tashjian, who extensively researched the tombstones of early New England, identified the Common Burying Ground in Newport, Rhode Island, as containing what may be the most surviving 18th-century headstones for African American graves. They look like other memorials of the time: "Just as Yankee artisans suppressed an African craft tradition, so too did the religious values of New England Puritanism prevail in the graveyard."[24]

In Lower Manhattan is the African Burial Ground National Monument. During construction for a federal office building in 1991, graves dating to the 1690s were discovered. They were identified as part of a burial ground located outside the city walls. A report from Howard University's New York African Burial Ground Project states that there "is no written record of the cemetery before 1712; however, a 1697 ban barring the burial of blacks, Jews and Catholics by Trinity Church suggests that the cemetery might have been created earlier than 1712 in response to a growing need for burial space."[25] An estimated 10,000 to 20,000 burials were conducted here by free and enslaved Africans and African

Americans who were not allowed to inter their dead in the churchyards, even when they had built the church, as in the case of Trinity. After the site was "rediscovered"—although it appears on old maps and in records and cannot have been called forgotten—activists pushed for its commemoration, leading to a museum and monument. These only cover a portion of what was the burial ground; remains are likely still beneath the surrounding blocks. Visiting the site, I noticed how the grave was emphasized in its design. Burial mounds are distinctive in the compact lawn, indicating where the remains from 419 people were reinterred in 2003. It cannot be experienced as an abstract monument.

This visibility is essential, but many other sites remain unmarked. On the Lower East Side, Manhattan's second major African American burial ground used from the late 18th to 19th centuries was located in what is now Sara D. Roosevelt Park. Although the burial ground was allegedly relocated to Brooklyn's Cypress Hills Cemetery in the 1850s, the neighboring New Museum now acknowledges in its site heritage that human remains were found during its construction in 2006.[26] It is remembered in public space only by the nearby M'Finda Kalunga Community Garden, its name in the African language of Kikongo, meaning "Garden at the Edge of the Other Side of the World." In Harlem, development at a former bus depot has raised questions about how the burial ground for enslaved and freed people beneath it that dates to the 17th century will be memorialized.[27] A Black cemetery in Port Richmond on

Staten Island held some 1,000 burials until it was seized in the 1950s due to unpaid property taxes. It was paved over and is now a strip mall.[28] There are others within New York City and many more beyond, the neglect of African American cemeteries persisting with a widespread lack of preservation and visibility.

A third burial ground near me is so hidden in Prospect Park that most runners and bicyclists who pass by on the adjacent road do not know it is there. A fence behind some trees allows a glimpse of a few headstones. While it may seem strange to have a cemetery in a public park, it was here first.

The Quaker Burial Ground was established in 1849 when the land was unused farmland.[29] Its nine acres cover a hill where some areas are landscaped, and others are dense with foliage. Members of the New York Quarterly Meeting and their families can still be buried or have their ashes scattered at the site. As a sign of humility for wealth or status, the tombstones are uniformly humble, and some graves are unmarked. It is open to the public only infrequently. Plants grow freely, birds perch without fear of dogs, and the sounds of nearby recreation are distant. In a park that sees heavy foot traffic, the cemetery is an ecological sanctuary.

The burial ground has its roots as a religious haven. The colonies were often unfriendly to the Quaker Friends, who, beginning in the 1650s, promoted a personal connection with God, a stance which diverged from the Church of England and its leadership. Many of the colonies passed anti-Quaker laws such as the Massachusetts General Court, which declared in 1656 that there was "a cursed sect of heretics lately risen up in the world . . . who take upon them to be immediately sent of God and infallibly assisted by the spirit."[30] Being (or befriending) a Quaker was sometimes punished with lashings or the cutting off of an ear, and a Quaker returning after being banished could be sentenced to death.

The Quakers who arrived in New Netherland faced this intolerance, as Peter Stuyvesant saw their spiritual meetings as a threat to the rigid structure of the Dutch Reformed Church. But they refused to leave. They set up a meetinghouse in 1696 on today's Liberty Place in Manhattan. This narrow street gets little light because of the closeness of the buildings on either side, but was once an open area where they buried congregation members in purposefully unmarked graves. As the city developed, burials shifted out of Lower Manhattan, and they moved uptown to a vault at Houston Street. On an early 1850s map created by mapmaker Matthew Dripps, the Quaker vault is one of eight burial grounds clustered into a few blocks; all but two are gone. Around the time the map was published, burials except in vaults or private plots were prohibited below 86th Street, leading to another exodus of the dead. Almost two decades before Prospect Park, the Quaker Burial Ground opened.[31] Rather than move again, they reached an agreement to remain.

But what of those other burial grounds on the Dripps map? The living and the dead have historically had an uneasy relationship in American cities. While in rural areas or on a family farm people could be interred close to home without too much trouble, in cities, the increasing density meant the dead were amid city life, sometimes literally. There are stories of graves spilling open into streets and basements. The constantly overturned dirt was not left fallow long enough for complete decay. Epidemics of cholera and yellow fever were blamed on these festering burial grounds where it was thought the miasmas—or bad air—could make you sick. Even Trinity, with its venerable New Yorkers like Alexander Hamilton, was considered for removal. Ultimately, its influential supporters prevailed.

The two of the Quaker's former cemetery neighbors that survive in situ—the New York Marble Cemetery and New York City Marble Cemetery (similarly named but distinct places)—were small-scale attempts to adapt to the regulations that had moved the dead out of Manhattan.[32] Each was designed with underground marble vaults to circumvent the ban on earthen burials, but together they only contained a few hundred graves. To keep up with the growing population—and its dead—the city would need a bigger solution.

The last in my necrogeography tour is the newest, the largest, and least obscure. It is the one where I have also spent the most time leading tours. Green-Wood Cemetery, founded in 1838, includes the highest point in Brooklyn and, like that mound in Tennessee, has a beautiful view overlooking the New York Harbor. It differs greatly from the colonial churchyard with its grim headstones, the Quakers with their austerity, and the long-invisible African burial grounds. It was one of many cemeteries created in the 19th century that forever changed the American grave. To learn more about this era, I left New York for Boston, where it all began.

3 THE LIVING AND THE DEAD

Even on a cold December day, the trees in the Consecration Dell at Mount Auburn Cemetery in Cambridge, Massachusetts, are full of birds. From a vernal pool in its center, steep slopes covered with foliage rise on all sides, making it feel more like a forest valley than a burial ground. On September 24, 1831, it was here that over 2,000 people gathered to witness the dedication of a radically new idea for the grave. No longer would the malodorous grounds—where bodies did not have a chance to decompose before the earth was opened to crowd in more dead—intrude on daily life. No more would tilting slate headstones adorned with skulls remind visitors of their inevitable rot. The landscape would be lush and green, the monuments would be uplifting, and the message of the tombs would not be one of facing the sardonic grin of death but of a glorious afterlife.

On that momentous autumn day, the crowd sat on wooden benches positioned around the Dell, which acted as a natural amphitheater. Together they sang a hymn written for the occasion by Reverend John Pierpont (who would, after his death in 1866, be interred nearby below a stately sarcophagus):

> Decay! Decay! 'tis stamped on all!
> All bloom, in flower and flesh, shall fade;
> Ye whispering trees, when we shall fall,
> Be our long sleep beneath your shade![1]

The *Boston Courier* remarked on the beautiful weather with an "unclouded sun and an atmosphere purified by the showers of the preceding night" and looked ahead to the "rambles of curiosity, health, or pleasure" in the cemetery.[2] Judge Joseph Story—another future Mount Auburn eternal resident—gave a consecration address, its message having a personal resonance as he had recently lost his ten-year-old daughter to scarlet fever: "These repositories of the dead caution us, by their very silence, of our own frail and transitory being. They instruct us in the true value of life, and in its noble purposes, its duties, and its destination."

It was a start fitting to the ambitions of Mount Auburn's founders, who envisioned a cemetery that was a garden, graveyard, and civic space all in one. "What's so dramatic about Mount Auburn is they made a burial space that was not just for the dead but for the living as well," Meg L. Winslow, the cemetery's Curator of Historical Collections and Archives, told me as we stood by one of the Dell trees where small birds flitted among the branches. "The burial grounds and the graveyards and boneyards were practical, functional spaces to bury the dead, but they weren't made to visit. This place was made to visit and learn from the plants that were being planted and from the inscriptions. It was bringing art and ornamentation to the landscape. That was a very intentional design."

Story said in his address that cemeteries "may be made subservient to some of the highest purposes of religion and human duty." Some of Mount Auburn's earliest monuments were not tombstones, but the kind of sculptures later erected in city parks. One by sculptor R. Ball Hughes is the first full-scale bronze cast in the country and depicts Nathaniel Bowditch, an astronomer and self-taught mathematician. Rather than mark his grave, which is at his family plot elsewhere in the cemetery, it was intended to inspire the living. This was unlike the earlier churchyards which startled visitors into mortal reflection.

As radical as Mount Auburn was, Winslow pointed out that if it had not opened, something like it would probably have been created because across the United States in increasingly crowded urban areas there was a need for a natural sanctuary and a new type of grave. Like many major American cities, Boston had experienced incredible growth with the acceleration of immigration in the 1820s, becoming an industrial hub. Along Boston's Freedom Trail, there are enough skull-adorned tombs from the city's early years to make even the most avid taphophile photographer exhausted (as I discovered on a sweltering summer's day). At the city's first graveyard, King's Chapel, an evocative

17th-century tombstone represents death with a skeleton wielding an arrow for the final blow as it attempts to snuff out life's candle, with Father Time futilely trying to hold back the inevitable. In Copp's Hill Burying Ground, planned in 1659, headstones with winged skulls lean in chaotic directions. In the Granary Burying Ground, established in 1660 to combat the overcrowding at King's Chapel, skeletons lounge on graves with scythes as if taking a break after a busy day of harvesting souls. The graveyards kept coming as the city expanded, with the Central Burying Ground added in 1756 and used until 1826.

As early as the mid-18th century, the people with their hands in this fetid earth—the gravediggers—were concerned. A March 10, 1740, petition presented by several gravediggers to the town selectmen stated that due to the lack of open space, they could only bury bodies four deep. It was becoming impossible not to break through to other graves when digging new ones.[3] In November 1795, a committee appointed to examine the burial grounds reported that, after consulting with physicians, the health of people in the area was "in danger from the crowded state of these Grounds, & the exhalations which must frequently arise from opening Graves therein."[4] Outbreaks of cholera, yellow fever, and other diseases were attributed to these unsavory spaces. In 1822, Mayor Josiah Quincy finally proposed that the city no longer allow new burials.[5]

Corpses are now known to not get people sick except in rare instances. The World Health Organization states, "Unless the deceased has died from a highly infectious disease, the risk to the public is negligible."[6] (There is a risk of illness if fecal matter from corpses gets into the water, however.) Yet cities like Boston saw a healthier city with the bodies further away and in a more pleasant locale. Some old burial grounds were soon reduced in size for new streets and construction. The *Bostonian* reported in 1895 that the new subway—the first in the country—was tunneling past the Central Burying Ground and turning up bones including a "skull, evidently that of a woman, the hair being fully three feet long, and as well preserved as on the day of burial."[7] Throughout the 19th century, the dead had to make way for the living.

What's known as the American rural cemetery movement of the mid-19th century was heavily influenced by what was happening in Europe. In densely populated cities, the dead were being moved to somewhere more hygienic and bucolic. Mount Auburn drew on the model of Père Lachaise in Paris, which opened in 1804. Before it was established, the graveyard situation had become especially dire in the Cimetière des Innocents, which had been taking in the dead since the 12th century. It was next to a busy market in Les Halles, where people selling wares were often stepping around fresh, shallow graves. It was unsustainable and unpleasant, and something had to change.

The first step was to get the centuries of bones out of these effluvious grounds, and it happened that another urban catastrophe solved this need. Below Paris are series of tunnels where calcium sulfate—or gypsum—had been mined since the days of the Roman city Lutetia. In the 1770s, these quarries had multiple collapses, even taking down parts of streets. When the Inspection Générale des Carrières examined the mines and went in to repair them against future calamities, the labyrinthine scale of these tunnels was mapped. Out of sight but easily accessible to a city that needed to rid itself of generations of corpses, it was the perfect place to relocate some bones. By the mid-1780s, remains from the Cimetière des Innocents and other old graveyards were being transported into the underground by night.[8]

Expressing interest in graves can lead you on some unexpected journeys, and on a May 2014 evening, I got a first-hand look at this realm of the dead. A friend invited me to a squat frequented by cataphiles, the avid explorers of the catacombs, and I joined a group of five adventurers who were more or less prepared. One of our members—the most experienced explorer who would blast EDM music for the whole visit—cracked open an ordinary utility cover in the sidewalk. With some fleeting thoughts that perhaps breaking the law so flagrantly in a foreign country was a bad idea, I followed down the ladder of metal handrails. The descent took us past electrical wires and other utilities for the world above until we finally reached a tunnel that required crawling on our knees.

On the other side, we were in the catacombs. Over the next few hours, we walked and scrambled past painted murals and other art created by previous visitors, such as alcoves with holders carved for candles and disused bunkers covered with graffiti. We paused at one point to examine a map by flashlight and I saw miles of tunnels on it snaking out in all directions. Some tunnels that we passed through were elegantly arched; others were so narrow they could just barely fit a person. One chamber nicknamed the "bone room" was filled with skeletal remains at a depth I could not tell. It was chaos, totally different from the orderly lines of bones in the catacombs section open to the public. Lying on my back and shining a flashlight up into a tall shaft, I could see where the bones had once been transferred into the underground from somewhere above and then had gotten clogged. It was like looking into the mouth of hell, and as I moved away, I heard a few clatter down, extremely thankful that none had fallen on my face and caused me never to sleep again. In the very early hours of the morning, we climbed out into a street and dispersed into the night.

It was a brief glimpse into the incredible scale of work that went into moving the grave out of the city center. The Paris Catacombs put the old bones out of sight; Père Lachaise offered a cemetery designed as much a garden as a burial ground, and other cities that had graveyard problems took note.

The Massachusetts Horticultural Society, founded in 1829, wanted to connect people with nature through an experimental garden and arboretum. General Henry A. S. Dearborn, its president, and Dr. Jacob Bigelow, its corresponding secretary, came together on a plan. They could create their garden by selling cemetery plots and, through this structure, design a place with the tranquility and grandeur of Père Lachaise. While there is little open greenspace in Père Lachaise where the narrow, chapel-like tombs crowd closely, Mount Auburn made the environment the focus. The graves were set back from the road, and paths were carefully planned and named for trees—linden, willow, spruce, cedar, fir, sycamore, and cypress. It was a place where people could not just experience nature but become part of it. Bigelow said in a lecture, in words that anticipated the modern green burial movement, that the "elements which have once moved and circulated in living frames, do not become extinct nor useless after death; they offer themselves as the materials from which other living frames are to be constructed."[9]

As Winslow described to me, walking through a cemetery like Mount Auburn is "filmic." Monuments were crafted in three dimensions to be experienced in the round, unlike the flat colonial tombstones usually carved on one side. A map of a rural cemetery is a knot of winding roads that makes any attempt to walk in a straight line futile. Like Central Park and other urban parks that would follow, each view was designed, with hills shaped and plantings placed as if brushstrokes in a living painting.

Different from what had come before, Mount Auburn was a huge success, and visitors arrived in droves to marvel at the sylvan place. On September 21, 1833, *The Evening Post* reported that the "Bostonians are getting up so beautiful a graveyard that there is some danger the living will seek a permanent residence within its borders."[10] Swedish author Carl David Arfwedson exclaimed after his visit, "Death inspires here no dread: on the contrary, a glance at this beautiful cemetery almost excites a wish to die."[11]

Instead of setting off a chain of experimental gardens, Mount Auburn was the prototype for a new American cemetery. Many others followed in quick succession, including Mount Hope in Bangor, Maine, in 1834; Laurel Hill in Philadelphia in 1836; Rose Hill in Macon, Georgia, in 1836; Green-Wood in Brooklyn in 1838; Green Mount in Baltimore in 1838; Spring Grove in Cincinnati in 1845; Elmwood in Detroit in 1846; Forest Home in Milwaukee in 1847; Oak Hill in Washington, DC, in 1848; Rosehill in Chicago in 1859; Homewood in Pittsburgh in 1878; and countless more all verdantly named. Almost every city was debuting its new home for the dead. In the dedication for Oakwood in Syracuse, New York, civic leader Elias W. Leavenworth declared it was a place to "commune with nature in her loveliest forms, and in these secluded retreats to forget for an hour the toils and cares of life."[12] (Apparently, the care of life that often comes up around death did not apply.)

"It's difficult to overstate how radical and influential these cemeteries were—the word cemetery wasn't even in our lexicon until the rural cemetery came about," said Nancy Goldenberg, the President of Laurel Hill and its sister cemetery West Laurel Hill in Philadelphia. "This was an era before there were municipal parks and those cemeteries served as sites where people would escape the center of cities to fresh air, to picnic, and to find a sense of relief from all the bustle and the grime of what was then a very industrial world. This was also a time before there was public sculpture, before there were art museums and galleries, and having these sculptures and monuments was something that people hadn't seen before."

Laurel Hill's founder John Jay Smith had been distressed by his visit to a crowded graveyard where he "found it impossible to designate the resting place of a darling daughter," leading him to "procure for the citizens a suitable, neat and orderly location for a rural cemetery."[13] As Goldenberg pointed out, even that word "cemetery" was novel; before there was the "burying ground," "burial ground," "graveyard," and "churchyard." The word "cemetery" was derived from the Greek *koimeterion* or "sleeping place" and sculptures of sleeping people were common, reinforcing this idea of death being a sleep from which one might wake in the next life rather than this harrowing moment of judgment for either salvation or damnation.

These cemeteries were mostly non-sectarian, although they drew heavily on Christian traditions. Their formation coincided with a religious transition wherein an early Christian emphasis on the corruption of the body and its inherent sin had shifted to messages of hope and resurrection. Movements like Spiritualism, where the dead were supposedly all around and just waiting for contact through mediums and seances, further contributed to designing cemeteries that supported relationships with the departed.

Although those with the largest plots and monuments were from the upper echelons of society, the rural cemeteries attracted a wider crowd who wandered on the weekends or made a stop as part of their travels. At Green-Wood, visitors could pick up souvenir stereoscopic images and hire a tour guide—cemetery tour guiding is an old trade. However, it wasn't always obvious to the public what to do in these new types of spaces that were neither open landscapes nor graveyards. As the *Long-Island Star* reported on October 17, 1839, the Common Council of Brooklyn had to pass an ordinance prohibiting the use of firearms in Green-Wood as visitors had "in several instance been put in imminent peril of life and limb" by people out on the hunt for wild animals.[14]

Temptation for reckless sportsmen aside, rural cemeteries were important places in establishing a heavily designed, idealized natural landscape that would influence the development of American public parks. They were almost always in or just outside cities, despite the "rural" in the movement's name. (Conversely, some practices in actually rural areas—like scraping the earth of vegetation in southern cemeteries—set cemeteries apart from the sprawling nature around them rather than bringing it close to the grave.) For a country that was still young, the cemeteries were a move away from European traditions to something distinctly American. In 1849, Andrew Jackson Downing, a pioneering landscape architect, asked: "does not this general interest, manifested in these cemeteries, prove that public gardens, established in a liberal and suitable manner, near our large cities, would be equally successful?"[15]

Many of the rural cemeteries have endured as respites for their cities. During the COVID-19 pandemic, there was an increased demand for them as outdoor space, especially in neighborhoods that lacked parks. As the founders of Mount Auburn envisioned, its landscape is continuing to offer consolation and calm.

By the time I left Mount Auburn, the sun was setting, making the brisk day frigid. There were still people walking in the twilight hours, in couples or alone, some with cameras or binoculars. I saw one solitary figure with an easel set up, painting a view to a hill of graves. On May 26, 1832, *The Liberator*, a Boston-based newspaper, published a short meditative piece in which the unnamed author writes, "I could not help thinking, while standing here, that the time may not be far distant when the stranger who visits Mount Auburn will lean over the wicket of my own grave."[16] And here I was, a stranger to the people buried in the ground, able to experience that same tranquility of nature shrouding the grave.

4 THE PRIVILEGE OF PERMANENCE

From the elevated tracks that clatter overhead, Most Holy Trinity Cemetery in Bushwick, Brooklyn, appears like any other Catholic cemetery established in the 19th century, with headstones, crosses, and angels arranged across the green grass. Entering the space reveals that, unlike most cemeteries where the markers are stone, these are metal. Although painted white or grey to resemble marble or slate, many are faded. Some are warped and rusted by time, others have sunk into the earth, and on a day with a breeze, some rattle and creak. According to the Most Holy Trinity Saint Mary Parish, this unusual choice of material meant "no distinctions were permitted to be made between the rich and the poor."[1] But a glance around the cemetery shows this didn't impede people from having bigger metal monuments, decorative statuary, or metalwork flourishes so their memorials stand out. Nothing, it seems, can stop the urge to make your grave a bit better than your neighbors. And with the expanded room for memorials in the cemeteries of the 19th century, there was a whole new landscape to fill with posthumous statements of wealth, power, and individuality.

A walk through a cemetery only presents one side of the grave; there are the underground burials and the interiors of the mausoleums as well. On a few of my cemetery tours, I've hefted long mausoleum keys that fit deep into huge granite doors that, if you're lucky, swing open with surprising ease. Some are relatively empty, just names on the marble crypts lining the walls. Others have tables, chairs, and kneelers—small acts of hope that someone would visit and break the silence. Some mausoleums are ostentatious shrines of wealth with chandeliers and Tiffany stained-glass windows; an exceptionally decadent tomb at Woodlawn in the Bronx has a pipe organ and was wired for electricity—never mind that there are no power lines in the cemetery. Some feel nice enough to live in. In fact, in Brooklyn's Cemetery of the Evergreens, a man named Jonathan Reed lived for a decade in the mausoleum where he interred his wife—outfitting it like a home complete with a stove and even bringing along their pet parrot—until he died there in 1905 and was buried with his love.[2]

The archives at Green-Wood in Brooklyn hold numerous blueprints for mausoleums, as detailed as the plans for any architecture. They don't appear that different from cross-sections of other buildings with the details on foundations and elevation. But a mausoleum has special needs; specifically space to hold the corpse. The dead are never visualized in these large blueprints, most of which date between 1910 and

1930. Some include underground vaults beneath the floor or individual above-ground crypts in the walls. Others have elaborate ornamentation such as glass mosaic vaults and gilt bronze elements, as well as features like vents, so the gases from decomposition have somewhere to go (and the smell of rot doesn't disturb any dutiful family visitors). These are graves designed to be solid, secure, and formidable.

The American mausoleum building heyday peaked in the first decades of the 20th century. One of the most impressive neighborhoods of these houses of the dead is Woodlawn in the Bronx. Taking the 4 train to the ominous end of the line and entering the gates, a visitor is awed by hundreds of colossal tombs, many larger than any apartment the average New Yorker can dream of living in. Woodlawn opened in 1863, and unlike Green-Wood, which required taking a ferry before the opening of the Brooklyn Bridge in 1883, it was accessible from Manhattan by train, making it the new favorite of the elite. Oliver and Alva Belmont chose it to erect their replica of the 15th-century St. Hubert Chapel in Amboise, France, where Leonardo da Vinci is said to be buried; the Woolworths of department store fame opted for a hulking Egyptian temple guarded by two busty sphinxes. Jules Bache, a banker and stockbroker, commissioned a duplicate of the Kiosk of Trajan, a temple on the Nile River with soaring columns topped with lotuses. Railroad magnate Collis P. Huntington built a massive double-flight staircase leading up to his gargantuan Classical Revival tomb—an imposing entrance based on Penn Station's steps.[3] Every detail was carefully selected down to the landscaping, the tomb a culmination of a lifetime of taste and a final place to show it off.

Railroad tycoon Jay Gould was interred in a Greek temple with columns on all sides, a towering weeping beech now growing by it like an oversize version of the weeping willow and urn that adorned countless churchyard tombstones. Curiously, his name appears nowhere on its exterior. The December 7, 1892, *New York Times* coverage of his funeral reported his casket was placed in a sealed "lead-lined oak box." After the mausoleum's hefty bronze doors were "securely locked," hired guards took their place outside so there would not be "any attempts at molestation."[4] A grand mausoleum in Woodlawn—removed from the crowded city—provided security even for someone who had made as many enemies as Gould, an infamous robber baron who shamelessly manipulated stocks and drove other businesses into the ground all to his profit. Historian Edwin Palmer Hoyt, in his 1969 book on the Gould family, observed that, "tomb vandalism was very much on the minds of millionaires," noting an especially gruesome incident in 1878 when the remains of merchant millionaire Alexander Turney Stewart were spirited from his grave and held for ransom.[5] Stewart had been dead for two years when his vault at St. Marks Church-in-the-Bowery was ransacked; two years later his widow finally paid $20,000 for bones that may or may not have been her husband's. Gould was not alone in his concerns. Stewart's grisly posthumous journey compelled

Levi Leiter of Marshall Field & Company to meticulously plan his mausoleum at Rock Creek Cemetery in Washington, DC. Concrete and steel beams secured the casket, and yet more concrete filled the chamber.[6] Neither Gould nor Leiter's eternal slumber has been disrupted in the fortress-like tombs they saw as one last worthy expense.

Grave robbing was a legitimate fear, although it was rarely the rich who were disturbed. While the churchyards were overcrowding and the wealthy were moving their graves out to idyllic gardens, American medical education was expanding. To better treat the living, medical students needed cadavers, and the demand regularly outpaced the supply. It was common knowledge that the source for the "resurrection men" who trafficked in these bodies was the graveyard.

An earthen burial offers little defense from a grave robber. While "six feet under" is a prevailing idiom for the grave, burials have frequently been shallower, especially in the older graveyards where the ground was already dense with bones. A strong rope around the corpse's neck and a determined pull were all it took to remove the body and dispatch it to the dissection table. Things got so tense in 1788 that the New York Doctors' Riot broke out. A medical student was said to have waved a severed arm out a window of the New York Hospital, yelling to a young boy below: "This is your mother's arm! I just dug it up!"[7] Whether an absolutely terrible joke or not, the boy told his father, and upon investigation, they discovered the mother's coffin was empty. A mob formed and stormed the hospital, where anatomical specimens were destroyed and medical students were forced to flee. The cavalry was sent in to quell the violence, and several people died. In the wake of the calamity, New York State passed a 1789 statute to supply executed criminals' bodies for dissection.[8]

Dissection has often been a punishment for executed criminals to further their sentence after their final breath. The Murder Act of 1752 in Great Britain stated that "in no case whatsoever shall the body of any murderer be suffered to be buried."[9] Denied the grave, many criminals are still in bits around museums, such as a head of a woman hanged in the 19th century in the Herbert Art Gallery and Museum in Coventry, England.[10] The skeleton of William Burke— hanged in 1829 for his role with accomplice William Hare in murdering people and selling their bodies for dissection—is at the Anatomical Museum at the University of Edinburgh. A pocketbook bound in his skin following his public dissection is in Edinburgh's Surgeons' Hall Museums.[11] The use of carceral bodies in dissection and display without consent continues today; the currently touring *Real Bodies* exhibition of preserved cadavers, some of which are presented as educational models while others are posed playing tennis or basketball, has regularly drawn concern that the bodies may be those of executed Chinese prisoners.[12]

Few were thus interested in donating their bodies with such stigma attached. Before philosopher Jeremy Bentham died in England in 1832 at 84, he made a statement by asking to be dissected. He initially drafted his wishes to give his body to science in a will he wrote in his early 20s back in 1769.[13] Specifically, he wanted to become what he called an "auto-icon"—a preserved human on display. (As one story goes, he carried the glass eyes he planned to have in his vacant sockets in his pocket to show off, surely a good conversation starter.) As a reformist and Utilitarian, he thought his corpse should be useful. He imagined that the widespread creation of auto-icons could replace statues which were mere facsimiles of great minds and leaders, while simultaneously existing to "diminish the horrors of death."[14]

Physician Thomas Southwood Smith followed his friend's wishes as best he could, dissecting Bentham's body and preserving his head with techniques he interpreted from the Māori in New Zealand and sulphuric acid. The head was an imperfect success, becoming a ghastly red color, but the skeleton was carefully dressed in Bentham's clothes, which were fleshed out with hay. The whole assembly was positioned sitting in a chair in a glass cabinet. In 1850, Bentham the auto-icon arrived at University College London (UCL), where he remains on view today, although with a less alarming wax head added by French artist Jacques Talrich.[15]

Bentham's strange "grave" has become an evolving interactive site with installations like a webcam called the Panopticam Project, referencing his idea of a panopticon prison where guards could monitor everyone from a single place (an improvement on order through physical brutality). In 2015, I visited him in London, where he still sits at UCL with his walking stick, wearing his big straw hat. I was surprised by how his large wooden box sat humbly in a hall where students walked past, his presence a part of the day-to-day flow of knowledge.

In his advocacy, Bentham also drafted an 1826 "Body-providing Bill," which he hoped could become legislation to address the need for legally dissectible cadavers.[16] Nevertheless, the practice of grave robbing—particularly in the most vulnerable burial grounds—continued and was hardly a secret. British surgeon Sir Astley Cooper infamously declared in 1828 to the Commons Select Committee that "here is no person, let his situation in life be what it may, whom, if I were disposed to dissect, I could not obtain."[17] (Cooper, for his part, was securely interred in 1841 in multiple coffins inside a stone sarcophagus.[18])

Some churches in the early 1800s in the United Kingdom and a few rare graves in the United States used devices called mortsafes that were forged from iron or had a hefty stone top.[19] They would rest on a newly filled grave until the corpse was too decayed to interest the resurrection men. Others weighed down their coffins so they would be hard to move, with recent excavation at the New Churchyard in London turning up an 18th-century coffin packed with sand and covered with rocks.[20] Burial clubs were formed to look out for one another. Others took more extreme measures. After Congressman John Scott Harrison (son of President William Henry Harrison and father of future President Benjamin Harrison) was stolen from his North Bend, Ohio, grave in

1878 and rediscovered by his family at the local medical college, fellow Ohioan Philip K. Clover patented a "coffin-torpedo" that would fire lead upon anyone trying to open the casket lid.[21] The Museum of Mourning Art at Arlington Cemetery in Drexel Hill, Pennsylvania—a magnificent collection of funerary history and oddities currently closed after auctioning many of its objects in 2016—had an early 18th-century "cemetery gun" designed to be set off by tripwires.[22]

The burial grounds often victimized were those of the poor and marginalized who could not afford or were not allowed protection for the grave. Those without access to mortsafes, grave guns, or mausoleums with locked doors were frequently buried the furthest from the safe proximity of a church or wealthy cemetery and sometimes could not watch over their dead at night. The African Burial Ground in Manhattan had curfew laws under the British, and mourners were barred from gathering in large groups.[23] A 1788 petition from Black freedmen—sent the same year as the Doctor's Riot—asked the city's Common Council to stop the blatant desecration of their burial ground where medical students "dig up bodies of our deceased friends and relatives of your petitioners, carrying them away without respect for age or sex."[24] Their plea was disregarded. DIY measures like leaving flowers or stones on the grave to indicate if it had been disturbed could only do so much. The March 3, 1827, issue of *Freedom's Journal*—the first African American-owned newspaper published in the United States—included a small item about "an easy way to secure dead bodies in their graves," advising that straw be "distributed in layers" with "every layer of earth," so that even on "the longest night" there would not be time to exhume the grave.[25]

This defilement of graves persisted throughout the country, and there was little legal protection for the dead. In 2018, the University of Virginia released its final report of its President's Commission on Slavery which included an examination of its medical school, finding that those most often dissected "at the University were largely the bodies of recently deceased African Americans (both enslaved and free)" and that they had been regularly stolen from their graves "for the school by hired professionals—known as resurrectionists."[26] The report describes how on December 10, 1834, a farmer named James Oldham, who owned land west of the school, heard his dogs barking. Going out into the moonlit night, he discovered five men digging up a grave where an enslaved person had been buried. Yelling at them to get out, he fired his gun at two who refused to leave, hitting one. The next day, a warrant was issued not for the grave robbers but for Oldham's arrest for shooting the medical student, a charge for which he was not indicted. The students' reaction to file a complaint that Oldham was in the wrong by disturbing their work reveals how grave robbing was seen as acceptable and necessary.

Legalizing the dissection of unclaimed corpses helped curtail the stealing of bodies for grave robbing, such as Massachusetts passing an anatomy act in 1831 and New York passing one in 1834. Still, it continued into the 20th century. Archaeologist James M. Davidson wrote in the *International Journal of Historical Archaeology* about evidence in Freedman's Cemetery in Dallas, Texas, that indicates the illegal dissection of Black cadavers dating from 1900 to 1907.[27] Permanency has always been a privilege in the grave, and that includes being able to rest undisturbed.

5 AN ETERNAL ROOM OF ONE'S OWN

In Arcadia, Oklahoma, on a summer day when a nighttime rain had left the ground soggy and the air humid, nature was flourishing in a 19th-century cemetery very different from those I had visited on the East Coast. Ferns and purple thistles sprouted between the graves, and small scrub oak trees grew on all sides. Snails crept over the rough fieldstone markers, and while standing in the tall grass trying to read the name on a handmade concrete monument, a tiny snake slithered over my shoe.

Gower Cemetery looks like any number of cemeteries situated on country roadsides, but its presence and survival represent a frequently overlooked history. This is a place created by a Black community to mourn and care for their dead in a way that had not been allowed in previous centuries.

John and Ophelia Gower joined the 1889 Land Run, which attracted a number of Black Americans, some who were previously enslaved, all hoping for a fresh start.[1] On their 160-acre homestead, the Gowers established this small cemetery for their family and others who settled in the vicinity. Later they opened it to anyone who needed a grave, including those who were unclaimed or unable to afford a plot elsewhere.[2]

A few hundred people are buried in Gower Cemetery, with the oldest marker dating to 1896. Ophelia, who died in 1922, has a sheaf of wheat on her headstone, symbolizing a life richly lived until the final harvest. Later her granddaughter, Myrtle L. Gower Thomas, advocated for preserving the cemetery, spearheading its 1991 listing on the National Register of Historic Places.[3] In a 1993 interview for the University of Central Oklahoma Oral History Project, Thomas said, "I don't like the fact that as I look around I see no symbols of African American heritage and their contributions to building the nation."[4] After she died in 2010, she was buried in the cemetery to which she had dedicated so much time, assuring its visibility.

Gower Cemetery is a rare Oklahoma site that preserves the presence of 19th-century Black homesteaders, and to be able to visit these graves is to remember them. The Oklahoma Constitution of 1907 did not include restrictive segregation to avoid a potential veto from President Theodore Roosevelt. But after it was officially a state, Senate Bill Number One— the very first bill, passed two weeks after statehood—was a Jim Crow law segregating transportation coaches and waiting rooms.[5] Segregation that had started in the previous century continued to expand over the following decades, including to cemeteries. Only in 2017, for instance, did a cemetery in Logan County, Oklahoma, finally, have a wire fence cut down that had segregated it since 1889.[6]

I grew up in Oklahoma and never heard of this heritage. When we studied the Land Run in high school history class, there was no mention of the Black people who joined, going somewhere they had never visited to have land that they would do with what they wanted, a powerful act with the abolition of slavery a recent memory. And the legacy of this cemetery in not only providing a place where their community could be buried, but where anyone could have a respectful grave is important. There is a monument indicating the grassy area where the "indigent" people who had nowhere else to go were interred. For those who died unclaimed or impoverished, their burials have long been precarious and often unmarked.

On a blustery day in early March 2020, the most haunting thing about being on Hart Island was not the crumbling structures leftover from asylums and quarantine hospitals or the trench partly filled with plain pine coffins. It was the ground. Everywhere the sandy soil was disturbed, with broken shells, bits of schist and quartz, and fragments of the abandoned architecture all churned together in the ongoing opening and closing of the earth to take in more than 1,000 burials each year. Nearby, the digging machines that excavate the land for this grim purpose sat idle, awaiting the Department of Correction (DOC) staff and inmates from the Rikers Island jail complex who conducted the burials, as they had for decades, on these shores.

This slender 131-acre landmass off the coast of the Bronx in the Long Island Sound is a potter's field. The term originates from the Gospel of Matthew, in which priests are deciding what to do with the silver left behind by the disgraced Judas before he killed himself: "And they took counsel, and bought with them the potter's field, to bury strangers in." Centuries of burial grounds ignored, overlooked, or considered sources of shame have been associated with this place purchased with the tarnished coin left behind by Judas.

Recently, oversight of Hart Island changed from DOC to the NYC Parks Department through four bills signed into law on December 4, 2019, by Mayor Bill de Blasio. This ended over 150 years of this island and its burials being under penal control. The inmate labor switched to contracted workers in early April 2020.[7] Those bills included authorization for plans to add more ferry access and an office to support public burial arrangements. Still, it's unclear how radically they will change the site, which remains sequestered.

You have to take a ferry to Hart Island from City Island, itself an oddity as it feels more like a New England fishing village than a neighborhood in the most populous city in the country. I was there that March day as a support mourner for a friend who was visiting Rosalee Grable, a rare person who asked to be buried there, choosing to be close to her mother even if it had to be in a mass grave where visitation through DOC could feel like accessing a prison. Phones and cameras had to be checked into a lockbox before boarding the ferry. It was a very short trip across the water, and stepping off the boat, we were greeted with small white stone angels and a statue of the Virgin Mary standing sentinel on some stones. A DOC-branded white bus with blue stripes and CORRECTION on the sides conveyed us to an area of both recent and older graves. A simple painted rock had been set on the dirt to mark her resting place.

No photographs were allowed—and I didn't have my phone or camera anyway—but a DOC employee took a souvenir polaroid, insisting on a backlit angle that obscured our features and made the grassless ground into a stark plane. I was there because I wanted to know what it felt like to visit the city's island of the dead. I had expected it to be somber; I hadn't anticipated the emotional weight of being where an estimated one million people have been interred and largely forgotten. The wind that ripped across the island was cold, and I left that troubled ground to wait in the bus, looking out the window towards a family visiting an uncle in a mass grave where coffins were visibly stacked. I thought about how the flowers they left for him would soon be blown away.

Just weeks later, COVID-19 would put Hart Island in international headlines as photographs of its mass burials conducted by people in hazard suits became searing symbols of the pandemic's toll. But what many who viewed them did not understand was that what they showed was not new, even if the number of bodies filling the ground was increasing. The way the dead were being placed in the anonymous layers was the same as it had been for decades. People just started paying attention.

Although it's a common superstition that it's bad luck to walk on a grave, the truth is those of us who live in urban areas likely pass over graves more than we know. A grave is not hard for cities to forget, especially if they largely forgot the people when they were alive. Remains of the potter's fields that preceded Hart Island in Manhattan often still linger with only scarce recognition. In City Hall Park, there is a granite marker, easy to miss on the edge of a lawn, that notes that during construction, remains from 18th-century burial grounds associated with an almshouse were found and reinterred. A smaller marker wedged below the original states that after those remains, even more were discovered and reburied in 2013. Renovations at Washington Square Park further uptown turned up several graves from when it was a potter's field and in 2009, a whole tombstone was discovered there for a man who died in an 18th-century yellow fever epidemic, a reminder that in times of mass death from disease even those who can afford a marker can end up in a mass grave.[8] In March 2021, staff from Green-Wood reburied a wooden box containing fragmentary remains in one of Washington Square Park's flower beds.[9] A paver near this site was installed to recognize the park as a mass grave where thousands were buried between 1797 and 1825, and their bones remain beneath the playground, dog run, fountain, benches, lawns, and paths.

Madison Square Park, Bryant Park, Wards Island, and Randall's Island were also New York potter's fields as the dead were pushed further and further out of the city. Then in 1869, Hart Island conducted its first burials, and the city's potter's field lost what visibility it had. In the 19th century, inmates from the penitentiary on Blackwell's Island (now named Roosevelt Island) dug and filled the graves; in the 20th century, it was Rikers Island.[10] For many years, little changed as the dead and the incarcerated moved between these islands nearly unseen.

Difficult to access and remote from much of the city, Hart Island regularly comes in and out of public consciousness. It's hard to know exactly how many people are buried there. Some records have been lost, including in a late 1970s fire.[11] To give an idea of the number interred in a non-pandemic year, according to the New York City Council, there were 1,213 individuals buried in 2018: 829 adults, 81 children, and 303 fetal remains.[12] The coffins are layered three deep. When a trench is closed, it has anywhere from 150 to 162 adult burials. For those that hold infant or fetal remains, it's 1,000.

From a prison camp for Confederate soldiers and a 19th-century charity hospital for women to a 20th-century drug rehabilitation program and Cold War Nike missile site, Hart Island has been a place for people and institutions the rest of the city did not want.[13] Through all these purposes, the consignment of the dead, including victims of epidemics, has also been relegated to the island. The first person recorded buried there in 1869—Louisa Van Slyke—died of tuberculosis at 24.[14] Later, in the 19th century, yellow fever patients were quarantined on the island; by the beginning of the 1900s, a tuberculosis hospital was on its shores. Early deaths from AIDS were isolated on the island's southern tip, buried under several feet more dirt than usual due to fear of the disease.[15] As explained by the AIDS Initiative of the Hart Island Project, a nonprofit that advocates for access and information about the site, since many funeral directors refused to collect the bodies of those who died of AIDS, they ended up among the unclaimed of Hart Island.[16] This was because of stigma as well as health warnings within the funerary industry. The *New York Times,* on June 18, 1983, reported that the New York State Funeral Directors Association had urged its members "not to embalm victims of AIDS."[17]

However they died, whether in a 19th-century cholera outbreak or the COVID-19 pandemic, the people in this mass grave are all democratized in this space. They do not have individual gravestones; concrete markers designate where hundreds of people are committed beneath the ground. If a name was recorded, it was written on the coffin in black permanent marker and is hidden in the earth. Because of the rules around visiting under DOC, they frequently go unmourned. Access gradually improved in recent years through the persistent advocacy of grassroots organizations such as the Hart Island Project and Picture the Homeless. There is now hope for better accessibility through NYC Parks. The only way anyone from the public without a connection to a mourner or a person buried on the island previously could visit was a once-a-month trip restricted to a gazebo—a generous name for a spare wooden shelter—built in the center of an empty field near the dock. There, a granite monument where stones and other mementos are left serves as a general memorial for thousands. It reads: "Blessed Are the Poor In Spirit For Theirs Is The Kingdom of Heaven." I joined one of these trips in 2016. For an hour, we could stand in the gazebo and look out on the quiet grassy lawn, and that was all.

Every place must manage the unclaimed, unidentified, and impoverished dead: the homeless, migrants who die far from their families, the elderly whose end-of-life care depleted their savings, people who outlived or were estranged from their kin, the stillborn, the unknown. Any of us could become one of them, alone at death and with no one to tend to our grave.

For such a universal need, there is no universal solution. Some states offer funding for burials or cremations by funeral homes; others have state, city, or local jurisdictions to manage these dead. There are no national statistics on the number of unclaimed or unidentified, and little data at the state level, further adding to their invisibility. Many of the laws relating to their processes can date to 19th-century anatomy acts initially instated to provide medical cadavers. The more recent laws have tended to be anti-abortion measures to impose a burial upon what many want disposed as medical waste. In 2019, for example, the Supreme Court upheld an Indiana law that mandated aborted fetuses either be buried or cremated.[18] A law like this is not engaging with the actual issue of unclaimed or unidentified remains.

Even where there are systems in place, the taxpayer money that funds them can be strained, as demonstrated by the COVID-19 pandemic and opioid epidemic. In West Virginia, escalating drug overdoses have regularly run dry a state program to support burials.[19] Maryland, where the State Anatomy Board takes unclaimed bodies for potential use in medical research, has likewise faced mounting numbers of the unclaimed linked to overdoses.[20] In 2010, budget cuts led Kansas to end its state-supported program for indigent burials.[21] Meanwhile, Cook County, which includes Chicago, appointed its first indigent coordinator in 2015 to address a significant backlog at its morgue by finding resting places for the deceased and tracking down kin.[22]

Unlike New York, most cities cremate unclaimed remains and store them in a medical examiner's office for a set time. The length they are there varies, as does their treatment after their time is up. Some can remain for as long as a decade, as is the case in Philadelphia; others have briefer periods in limbo, such as in Los Angeles, where it's three years.

After the hourglass runs out, they often do not receive a permanent resting place. In North Carolina, cremated remains are stored for three years and then scattered at sea.[23] In Pierce County, Washington, the unclaimed from the medical examiner's office are scattered in Puget Sound.[24] A few cities have gatherings where the dead are remembered and sometimes receive a collective marker. In Los Angeles in 2021, the Burial of the Unclaimed Dead interfaith ceremony was held for its 125th year, with 1,780 people who died in

2018 buried at Evergreen Cemetery in a plot owned by Los Angeles County.[25] The annual event inters the cremated unclaimed from the morgue and coroner's office in a shared grave with a marker simply carved with the year. Similarly, in Philadelphia's Laurel Hill, a stone is inscribed: "1,500 citizens consigned to earth, City of Philadelphia, 2010."[26] Each year at Springfield Hospital Center in Maryland, ashes from the bodies sent to the State Anatomy Board are interred at a shared marker reading: "This monument has been placed with deep appreciation for those who gave unselfishly of themselves to advance medical education and research."[27]

Some nonprofits have stepped in to fill the void, although they usually specialize in certain groups. The Garden of Innocence, which has several locations mainly in California, supports memorials for unclaimed and unidentified children. The Missing in America Recovery Project started in Idaho focuses on unclaimed veterans. On Staten Island, the Foundation for Dignity established in 2014 specifically states one goal: that no Staten Islanders will "be relegated to Hart Island."[28]

On March 7, 2020, on Hart Island, I had no idea that things would soon so radically change. A few days before I had idly tweeted a *New York Magazine* article titled "How Will New York City Respond to the Coronavirus?" published alongside the state's first confirmed case, noting as "a last resort" the city would have overflow burials on Hart Island.[29] Just a month later, Reuters reported that about 24 bodies were being buried by contract laborers each day as opposed to the around 25 ordinarily interred in a week.[30] It was and will be a place forever associated with the pandemic. Research published by *THE CITY* with Columbia Journalism School's Stabile Center of Investigative Journalism on March 24, 2021, stated that New York City was "on pace to inter one in 10 of its COVID-19 victims in the potter's field."[31]

Even after wave after wave of COVID-19 has coursed through the city, I wonder if Hart Island will be forgotten again until another tragedy pulls it into focus. And there will again be the shock and outrage, but no real change for how we care for our most vulnerable dead.

As we rode back to the ferry on the DOC bus that day in March, we saw two deer bounding through the long grass on an area of the island not currently being excavated for burials. For all that this place means to the city's problematic past and present care of the dead, it can also be beautiful. There are ospreys that nest by the dock and wildflowers that emerge from the earth when it's left alone long enough for seeds to grow. There are trees that line the roads and views to the water where sailboats bob in the currents. More landscaping could heal the broken ground. If it became somewhere people could easily visit and see, could it be a place where people would choose to be buried? In 2016, I spoke with Melinda Hunt, the artist who founded the Hart Island Project, about its potential to be a green burial site, something the city lacks. With the pine coffins, lack of embalming, and burial in the earth, it is already practicing natural interment. She noted that when people can be buried close to where they lived, there's more community care about those graves.

In 2015, the Hart Island Project launched the Traveling Cloud Museum, which visualizes over 73,000 burials on the island since 1980.[32] Clicking a plot number from an aerial view opens the names of the dead; sometimes they are just "Male Unknown," but for others, there is a name and their story, often contributed by family members, confronting the myth that this is an island of the unloved. The map now has color-coded numbers for AIDS and COVID-19 deaths, which cluster together in sections, recalling when the deaths were highest and kept coming. Similar to how green burial grounds use GPS for unmarked graves, there is potential to use this technology for Hart Island and build on these visibility efforts.

In the past decades, few major cities have added new cemeteries or columbaria. To purposely reimagine a place so long ignored as somewhere people would welcome being interred could honor the departed and offer a grave for those who need a final place to go. For now, Hart Island's future remains unclear, but the bodies will remain part of its ground forever.

6 NO RESTING PLACE

Designers Massimo and Lella Vignelli did not include a columbarium in their 1977 work on Manhattan's Saint Peter's Church. Amid the frenetic movement of Midtown, they created a sanctuary of stillness within the triangular church that has a distinctive granite roof sloping in the Citigroup Center skyscraper's shadow. From the layout of the interiors to a processional cross and the cushions on the pews, they gave every detail modernist lines and harmonious colors from elegantly functional materials like red oak and steel.[1] It was a fitting and thoughtful design for a congregation that was passionate about the arts, music, and community.

When AIDS became a crisis in the 1980s, the parish became a place of support, including through the founding of the Momentum Project, which centered its social services around a home-cooked meal. Social worker Peter Avitabile organized the outreach program, and it helped fill caregiving and counseling gaps for anyone in need and offered companionship and community at an isolating time. One unnamed man told the *New York Times* in May 1986, "You can feel like a human being here."[2]

Especially in its early days, AIDS was a disease that meant death. As funeral directors were turning away people who died from it and workers in burial and cremation were reluctant to handle their bodies, having a dignified final resting place became part of the care at St. Peter's.[3] Some partners of the deceased had not been allowed in the hospital rooms; others had died alone without their families who refused to visit.

A conversation at the church about a columbarium led to contacting the Vignellis. They were not only enthusiastic about making this addition but requested to be inurned there as well. It was dedicated on Transfiguration Sunday of 1993.

"The church wanted to provide a place where people could be sheltered, to be in community and remain in community, even in death," Pastor Jared Stahler told me as we stood in front of the columbarium where some of those lost to AIDS were at the center of a grid of muted stone.

Stahler observed how its minimal design—constructed by Eickhof, a company that engineers and builds columbaria—was guided by the Vignellis's adherence to thoughtfully distilling an object to its essence through geometric forms. It is a perfect double square of 4x4 panels, with each panel containing 3x3 niches. If a name and date—written in the Vignelli-approved typeface Optima—were too long to fit on two lines, rather than centering the text, another line is added to descend like the nearby organ pipes, themselves contained within a larger square. The columbarium also echoes the square arms of the pews with their square cushions and the square baptismal font. Massimo, who died in 2014, and Lella, who died in 2016, are now in niches at a top corner.

"I look at these names, and they're from across the whole community," Stahler said, pointing out people who died of HIV/AIDS, Momentum volunteers, jazz musicians who performed in the sanctuary, clergy associated with the church, and members from when St. Peter's merged with Iglesia de Sion. One congregation member who died in the 9/11 terrorist attacks has a niche containing only her shoes. There are also recent COVID-19 losses.

"There was a question about, 'what you do with a body that has died of HIV?'" Stahler said. "It was not dissimilar, in a sense, from some of the things that we've seen with COVID-19 and people who are looking for the dignity of human burial."

Much of the columbarium is now full. It may not be expanded and will instead stay as it is, recognizing 30 years of people mourned in a congregation and the moments in which they lived and died.

"I've begun to wonder, 'is this what was the faithful response in a certain period of time?'" Stahler said. "And then the question becomes, 'what's the next response?' My heart has wondered, do we honor these people and this time? And does this become something greater than just an individual resting place?"

He described how in the Good Friday Passion presentation, a cross is draped with a red cloth that becomes a shroud, the cross acting as a stand-in for a body. It is processed up to the columbarium and placed below these names. At this moment, they are not just individuals, but a reminder that death touches everyone, and everyone is deserving of dignity at the end.

Around the time St. Peter's added its columbarium, ACT UP was staging Ashes Actions, including in 1996 when cremated remains of people who died from AIDS were thrown onto the White House Lawn.[4] It was an extreme action that couldn't be ignored, driven by rage at government neglect; here were the dead and only the ashes left of them. It was a call for the country to grieve.

Cremation allows the dead to be mobile and remembered outside the cemetery. They can stay in a community as at St. Peter's or be transformed into symbols, objects, or dispersed to the wind. It was only in the 20th century that it became a common disposition option in the United States. Yet it is one of the oldest rituals of the grave dating back at least 40,000 years to New South Wales, Australia, where the remains of a woman known as the Mungo Lady were discovered. Her body was cremated and ritually buried.[5] It has been a traditional funerary rite in the Hindu, Sikh, and Buddhist religions for thousands of years. Although there are tombs after tombs adorned with draped urns in Victorian cemeteries, rarely were any of the people below cremated. It had fallen out of favor in much of Europe and the United States and even became a taboo. The Catholic Church condemned it in 1886, and it took until the 1960s for the Church to approve it again.[6] It would take a strange journey through funerary experimentation to bring cremation into the American mainstream.

No teenager had greater gloom than when a 17-year-old William Cullen Bryant advised in his 1811 poem "Thanatopsis":

> By an unfaltering trust, approach thy grave,
> Like one who wraps the drapery of his couch
> About him, and lies down to pleasant dreams.

Not until six decades later would he be shrouded in that final slumber. On May 29, 1878, an 83-year-old Bryant gave remarks in Central Park at the unveiling of a bust honoring Italian patriot Giuseppe Mazzini.[7] His friend General James Grant Wilson later recalled noticing that the aged poet appeared weak, struggling to find his place in his notes, but by the end reclaimed his old power and, facing the bronze, declared, "Remain for ages yet to come where we place thee, in this resort of millions."[8]

Wilson insisted on walking his friend to his home, and together with Wilson's young daughter, they strolled through the park, noticing statues of men Bryant had known—Fitz-Greene Halleck, Samuel Morse—now dead and immortalized. ("I prefer the portraits of me in old age," Bryant remarked, considering the youthful depictions of some of his contemporaries.) They made it to the steps of Wilson's house, then Bryant suddenly fell, hitting his head.[9] He never recovered and died days later, on June 12.

Bryant would be buried in Long Island's Roslyn Cemetery beneath an obelisk that is tastefully not too tall. With the foresight of one with death long on the mind, he'd bought the cemetery's first plot in 1861.[10] The corpse of Mazzini—the man who he extolled with his last public words—had a stranger fate and was turned to stone by someone who would revolutionize the modern grave and unmoor it from the cemetery through the revival of cremation.

Paolo Gorini detested sepulchral decay, writing in 1876, "What happens in burial is beyond comparison sadder and more repugnant than what would have happened to the body left on the ground," calling the grave a "subterranean prison."[11] The Italian scientist dedicated time between 1843 and the 1870s to perfecting a process for petrifying the human corpse.[12] Unlike funerary embalming, this preservation had an edifying intent. He considered that famous people could be preserved for the "admiration of posterity."[13] Results of his secretive methods are still on view in the *Collezione anatomica Paolo Gorini* in Lodi, Italy, where visitors can see heads, hands, and a whole body with stone-like skin.

Mazzini, who died in 1872, and the novelist Giuseppe Rovani, who died in 1874, were among the handful of bodies on which Gorini tried out his petrification techniques. However, they were both ultimately interred in ordinary graves beyond the sight of potential posthumous admirers.[14]

Alongside these experiments, Gorini came upon the idea for cremation cataclysmically in April 1872. The Italian government had commissioned him to write about the origins of volcanoes and he was investigating lava's properties. He noticed that insects that had the misfortune to fall into his incandescent crucibles vanished into flame; "[t]his made me think that the same thing could happen with any animal matter, including different parts of the human corpse."[15]

Gorini's human sculptures may have been ahead of their time—the *Body Worlds* exhibitions were still over a century away—but he found a much wider audience for cremation. Following his insect immolations, he designed a crematorium with cremation proponents Agostino Bertani and Gaetano Pini for the Cemetery of Riolo in Lodi. There, the dead were wheeled into a large oven where they were consumed by flames from a wood-fired furnace.[16] It was Italy's first modern crematorium and was completed in 1877. It's where Gorini himself would be cremated rather than turned to stone after his death in 1881.

The "Gorinian" crematorium became popular and spread throughout Europe and to the United States. Along with this rise of death innovation, the crowding that led to the rural cemetery movement also sparked the interest in cremation. Some advocates argued it was more hygienic than burial. In 1874 in *The British Medical Journal,* William Eassie, a member of the Cremation Society of Great Britain, described "the revolting sites I witnessed when a boy in some Lancashire churchyards" and wondered "how it has come to pass that we practise burial with its many faults, and do not burn our dead." Although he noted the improvements offered by the new cemeteries on the outskirts of London like

Kensal Green and Tower Hamlets, he observed "that a proper site for a cemetery is not everywhere obtainable" and ones close to homes and water sources still posed the dangers and unpleasantness of the boneyards.[17]

The first crematory in the United States opened in 1876. Pennsylvania physician F. Julius LeMoyne erected the brick one-story building as he believed it a more sanitary way to go. To many, LeMoyne's passion for a cleaner death made him an oddball rather than a pioneer. When he died, his obituary crowed, "The Eccentric Physician's Body Burned in his own Furnace."[18] The facility cremated just over 40 bodies before closing in 1901.[19]

Cremation was slow to catch on. While spurred by the belief in a more hygienic way to dispose of the dead, the mass death of the early 20th century would further change America's relationship to the cemetery and lessen the excesses within them. With thousands dying in the two world wars and the 1918 to 1919 flu pandemic, there was little interest in constantly donning the widow's weeds, building the marble angels, and picnicking at the graves. People also moved around the country more frequently, lessening demand for family plots where generations would lie down together.

Between 1960 and 1969, cremation increased from 3.5 percent of dispositions to 4.5—a slight but steady rise. A *New York Times* story on the uptick cited reasons ranging from cost to shifting religious beliefs, although it was "still largely limited to the white, upper middle class."[20]

It wasn't until 2015 that cremation would outpace burial in the United States, and it has continued to grow.[21] According to the Cremation Association of North America, the cremation rate was 56.1 percent in 2020, up from 54.6 percent the year before.[22]

Cremation could have ended the grave as a place, but often these remains—or "cremains" as they are regularly referred to in the United States as a step away from the more elemental "ashes"—still have a permanent location. Some are buried in conventional graves, frequently as part of a family plot. As with the wall of niches at St. Peter's, it is powerful and often important to have a place where a person can be remembered and celebrated. In 2014, I walked through the many rooms of Oakland, California's Chapel of the Chimes. It resembles a Tuscan church with its Romanesque bell tower. Inside, stained glass windows and skylights illuminate a labyrinthine series of atriums, chapels, and courtyards filled with shelves of urns behind glass and muttering fountains, small gardens, and Gothic arches. It feels more like a cloister or library than a columbarium; some urns are even shaped like books. The sensation of ethereal calm is thanks to a 1928 redesign by Julia Morgan, an architect who was an expert in bringing a feeling of history into 20th-century buildings, including in her best-known work at Hearst Castle.[23] Similar to the rural cemeteries, it was designed to be a place for the living and the dead. It's a rarity. Most of the 20th and 21st-century columbaria were additions within cemeteries and sometimes as unimaginative as a freestanding wall. There have been few instances in the United States of architects and designers thinking of what a place just for cremated remains could look like and how it could differ from a cemetery.

Cremation allows the grave to be anywhere and almost anything. Over a century after Gorini's machine, there are staggering options for transforming ashes into memorial objects. There are fireworks mixed with ashes, vinyl records pressed with ashes that play the voice of the departed, hourglasses where the sands of time are remains, diamonds made from the carbon of the deceased, portraits painted with ashes, tattoos with ink made with ashes, and biodegradable urns that grow into trees. There are eternal reefs where ashes are combined with concrete for porous structures installed on the seafloor as marine habitats. The most extravagant is the Neptune Memorial Reef, opened in 2007 off the coast of Florida's Key Biscayne. It is planned to cover 16 acres with columns, arches, and underwater sculptures, including starfish, seashells, and even a lion.[24]

There are also services to launch remains into space or near-space. Cremated remains have voyaged into space since 1992 when the ashes of *Star Trek* creator Gene Roddenberry rode on NASA's Space Shuttle Columbia.[25] Researcher Eugene Shoemaker, an outer-space collisions expert who worked on Moon Ranger missions, got an appropriate send-off when a small vial of his ashes road on NASA's Lunar Prospector science craft as it plummeted into a moon crater at 3,800 mph in 1999, making him the first person to have their remains resting somewhere extraterrestrial.[26] Thirty grams of ashes from astronomer Clyde Tombaugh were put on the New Horizons spacecraft, which in 2015 passed by Pluto, the dwarf planet he discovered in 1930 at the age of 24. The spacecraft has the power to keep operating through the 2030s, with Tombaugh going deeper and deeper into space.[27]

The litany of creative cremated remains uses goes on. Even if the market for, say, a posthumous fireworks display is probably small (although Americans love fireworks), it gives people more control over how they want to be remembered. Still, the dominance of cremation has led to concerns over its environmental footprint, including the fossil fuels it requires and how the burning of the things we carry in our bodies like mercury dental fillings can have a negative impact. The United Nations' Global Mercury Assessment reported that cremation emissions were about 3.77 tons in 2015, which is tiny compared to gold mining or cement production, yet raises questions about how its growth could affect the world.[28] There have been ideas for harnessing the energy from cremation. In Scandinavia, some crematoria are designed so the excess heat can warm a chapel or other building, but moves to connect that heat to local systems have been met with debate over if it is ethical and what it means to turn an individual's cremation into a commodity.[29]

It's also a process that can feel distant and abstract, as unlike cremation in other parts of the world, such as how it is practiced in Hinduism, it is not regularly witnessed in its industrialized form. Only in Crestone, Colorado, can the American dead be cremated on an open-air pyre instead of in a machine. (And there, it's only open to residents or property owners.) With these environmental concerns and the desire for more involvement from loved ones, others are looking at a return to another ancient but long unconventional funerary system for the United States: simply putting bodies into the ground and letting death be a new beginning of life through decomposition.

7 TO DECAY OR NOT TO DECAY

The Manhattan skyline is faintly visible from a hill in Sleepy Hollow Cemetery, but the burial ground north of the city feels like a world away. There is a whole history of remembering the dead here, beginning with the Old Dutch Church that connects to the cemetery's southern edge. The church and its churchyard, founded in the late 17th century, are referenced in Washington Irving's story, "The Legend of Sleepy Hollow" and the spooky feel is enhanced by a gathering of reddish-brown headstones where winged souls preside over ominous epitaphs. Like other colonial churchyards, this is a place where the way of all flesh is without question, and the repeating reminders of life's brevity are intertwined with an urgency to consider your eternal fate. ("Repent in time while time you have / There's no repentance in the grave," one headstone chimes in.)

The ground slopes upward north of the church, past Irving's family plot that becomes a pumpkin-adorned destination around Halloween. Irving was passionate about establishing the cemetery during the rural cemetery movement, relocating his family from their vaults at the Brick Church in Manhattan when they were threatened by development.[1] He even suggested the name Sleepy Hollow to imprint his legend on the landscape, writing that it would "secure the patronage of all desirous of sleeping quietly in their graves."[2]

The tombstones get newer over the hill, with 19th-century marble angels and granite markers within family plots sectioned off with metal fences and the old Dutch names only sporadically seen. Then, past formidable oaks and tall white pines are gargantuan monuments from the early 20th century. William Rockefeller has a hulking classical revival mausoleum lined with ionic columns; John Dustin Archbold put some of his Rockefeller wealth from Standard Oil into a huge domed tomb with a glass mosaic ceiling.

Although the cemetery is a little older in places and often extravagantly monumental, this rhythm of time and tombstones is akin to most American cemeteries. But nestled along one road is something different. At first, this section appears empty and unremarkable, with a couple of rustic benches positioned below the evergreen trees. Yet in this simplicity is a radical return to the past that does away with now-conventional practices of the grave.

This is Sleepy Hollow's Riverview Natural Burial Grounds. It is just a sliver of the cemetery, but it provides a rare opportunity in a modern American cemetery: to be buried in the ground with no metal, concrete, or hardwood barrier between your body and the soil. Everything that goes into the earth here must be biodegradable or natural, including the shroud, casket, or urn.[3]

I visited this spot in January 2022 when the temperature was well below freezing, and a thin layer of snow had turned to ice on the long, golden grass. I didn't notice the headstones until I was walking through the space. They were flush to the ground, many made from rough stone. Some had recently been visited and were wrapped in evergreen boughs or pebbled with small rocks or shells. The symbolism was more eclectic than in the rest of the cemetery—trees of life, a rabbit, a lotus flower, and a bicycle alongside the epitaph "It'll Be Okay." Some had verses from Robert Frost or Shakespeare; others spoke to the diverse backgrounds and beliefs of the people interred, including a Star of David and writing in Chinese and Cyrillic characters. Each felt incredibly personal, but the most personal statement was that they chose to be buried here instead of across the road.

I sat down on one of the benches, listening to the murmur of the Pocantico River nearby. I noticed hoof tracks pressed into the snow. Walking out of the cemetery later, through the more familiar upright headstones, I startled two young white-tailed deer bucks, also wandering through the graves. It wasn't quite like being out in wild nature—especially since a roadway rushes by the cemetery entrance and the Metro-North train station is a stone's throw away—but it was peaceful, and the green burial area had an extra reflective calm.

Sleepy Hollow is the closest place to me certified by the Green Burial Council (GBC), a green burial education and outreach nonprofit that sets standards for voluntary certification of green burial grounds. Over the past century, cemetery regulations have regularly required concrete liners to prevent graves from sinking or collapsing, leading to an uneven lawn. Funerary marketing has promoted pricey hardwood and steel caskets with synthetic liners. And with a limited number of green burial sites, interment in just the earth can be inaccessible.

What a green burial looks like varies widely, but at its core, it's a grave with as minimal an impact on the environment as possible. Some green burial grounds are "hybrids" at cemeteries like Sleepy Hollow that also practice conventional burial. Much like the way cemeteries incorporated cremation alongside conventional burial, green burial is being added, with Mount Auburn in Cambridge and West Laurel Hill in Philadelphia among those certified as hybrid cemeteries by the GBC.[4] Other sites exclusively devoted to green burial are restoring forests with plans to conserve the grounds as a natural area. What's considered the country's first conservation burial ground opened in Westminster, South Carolina, in 1998. Billy and Kimberley Campbell founded the Ramsey Creek Preserve to protect woodlands from development through the presence of graves, with the sales of plots funding conservation efforts. As of December 31, 2021, seven conservation cemeteries in the United States were certified by the GBC.

Some allow markers; others do not. Some people decide to be cremated before they are interred in a green burial ground. Many places have "burial ground" in their name, a return of attention to what is below after the rise of "cemetery" in the 19th century shifted the focus to the surface.

If I wanted to be buried in a forest, my closest option is in Rhinebeck, New York, about 100 miles north of New York City. A few years ago, the town's cemetery was unremarkable from any other conventional cemetery in the state. Its burials date to the 19th century with the resulting mix of Victorian monuments and modern granite headstones. Then, in 2014, Rhinebeck opened its natural burial ground.[5] It is a small area with about 2.5 acres surveyed for burial and is accessed by a walking path. It looks entirely different from the rest of the cemetery as it's located in a young forest on former pastureland with slender pines, maples, and oaks. Markers are optional and must be flat and made of stone local to the Hudson Valley, so they blend into the landscape.

"People are visiting all the time, just to use the space to walk," Suzanne M. Kelly, the cemetery's administrator, told me. "Cemeteries have historically been places where people used them as parks."

Along with being a farmer, Kelly is a green burial advocate. She helped create this municipally operated green burial ground as Chair of the Town of Rhinebeck Cemetery Committee. She explained that in New York State, when a nonprofit cemetery closes, a municipality takes it over. These kinds of cemeteries are often minimally maintained. After the committee took over the cemetery in 2002, Rhinebeck returned to its roots. Kelly noted that the older part of the cemetery was almost certainly green at some point since it started in 1835, before embalming, hardwood caskets, and vaults were the norm. The woods in the dedicated natural burial ground would likely have been cut down to make more room for the lawn-style graves if the area had not been transformed. Now people can choose whether they want a conventional or natural burial at the cemetery.

Although a carriage road accesses the green burial ground, it's gated off to cars. For Kelly, a low-impact human presence is essential.

"Green burial reconnects us to the land," she said. "Unlike, say, our national parks, even though people go to large swaths of those spaces, nobody lives there. We took people off the land to allow people to sometimes visit the land. And it's done a great deal in terms of protection, but in terms of conservation, do we mean conservation apart from human presence? Green burial tries to rectify that by literally putting somebody in the woods, saying humans belong to the space, and so do the living who want to visit those spaces. We can also care for the land by being on the land."

Many American funerals end at the graveside, and the mourners leave before the body is lowered and covered by backhoes and other machines. In a green burial, the interment is frequently a communal process. Lee Webster, a home funeral and green burial advocate, pointed out that when there is a closer connection between loved ones and the grave, there's heightened communication with the funeral director, cemetery workers, and others involved, making it all part of a collective ritual of care.

"I was helping a family about a month ago who had done a home funeral after hospice, and then did a home burial, which is legal in all states," Webster said. "And the difference between the experience for the family and their friends and the broader community is just night and day." She continued,

> With cremation, somebody dies, they come back in a box, and you might have a memorial. With green burial, you are in the moment. You have to process it; you have to absorb it. You have to do this within community, within family. As opposed to conventional burial, you're not just driving in to watch something on top of indoor-outdoor carpet. You're actually carrying your loved one into the grave. You're filling the grave afterward. You're touching it and being there with other people.

When I talked to Nancy Chubb and Laura Faessel of Forest Natural Burial Park, Pete McQuillin had recently passed away on January 8, 2022. McQuillin and his wife, Chubb, had opened the 35-acre site outside of Pittsburgh in 2011 because they wanted a place for an environmentally friendly interment and could not find it.

"We were having one of those couple conversations that are like, 'well, when I die, I just want my body to go into the earth,'" Chubb said. "So we googled green burial and found the closest green cemetery at that point was in Ithaca, New York. And I said there are probably other people like us who want to be buried this way. We didn't know anything about cemeteries; we just knew this sounded like a great idea of what we wanted."

Before acquiring the land, they started the nonprofit Green Burial Pittsburgh in 2008 to see if others were interested. Chubb noted that green burial "does kind of cross that blue-red divide," as both people drawn to ecological causes and hunters who want a burial in the woods are interested. Penn Forest now includes a Jewish area as the religious traditions of burial in a plain coffin or shroud align with the tenants of green burial. One of their disposition choices is "Treemation," where cremated remains are buried below a tree native to Southwestern Pennsylvania.

In addition to creating a place where they could envision themselves resting eternally, McQuillin and Chubb wanted to restore former pastureland into a forest. Only a part of the grounds are planned to be used for burials, with a third kept wild as a nature preserve.

"We have 35 acres, and a little over three and a half right now are used for burials," said Faessel, Penn Forest's manager. "There are also hiking trails, a flower picking garden; there's a farm with goats and sheep, a donkey, and ducks. We do yoga with goats whenever the weather's nice."

Although Chubb said these activities weren't in their original plan, they align with making green burial and death something that people are more open to talking about and contributing to a place that's ultimately "about life." The young trees planted in the recent burial areas will grow over time. Someday, when burials have stopped, and the land is at capacity, it will be a natural sanctuary. A portion of the sales from the lots goes to an endowment for this long-term care for the land.

Loved ones can participate in every step of the process, including digging the grave, carrying the casket, and lowering it into the ground. I watched Pete McQuillin's burial on Zoom, his shrouded body visible on the screen as people shared their memories. "It was very strange to put Pete in the ground," Chubb told me. "The whole point of the cemetery was so that we could be buried here. From just one of those couple conversations about what I want when I die, we built this amazing place with all these amazing people." The memorial ended with McQuillin being lowered into the earth and everyone there taking turns filling the grave, each helping to make his final wish come true.

After over a century and a half of the grave moving out of cities and becoming removed from the decay promised by those skeletal faces on the colonial headstones, the connection between the dead and the land has been disassociated from the cemetery. Green burial remains out of the mainstream—there are tens of thousands of conventional cemeteries compared to hundreds of green burial grounds. It is more common to be embalmed and buried surrounded by a grave intended to limit contact with the earth.

Mummification to arrest the putrefaction of the corpse has centuries of history. Yet unless you lived in an arid place, such as the Atacama Desert in Chile—where the Chinchorro people beat the ancient Egyptians to mummification by 2,000 years—the complex process was usually reserved for the elite.[6] So were other designs in the grave to resist decay; in China, during the Han Dynasty, intricate burial suits made of square pieces of jade, a stone with magical associations believed to preserve the flesh, covered the bodies of royalty.[7] For everyone else, the moldering of the corpse was something to be dealt with rather than stopped.

Burial happened quickly in the early years of the United States. Measures like a cooling board—a perforated wooden surface that held the corpse above ice—could help keep the body from decomposing for a short time, whether to wait for a funeral or for the ground to thaw in winter. But eventually, the body was always relinquished to the elements and the earth.

That changed in the 19th century in large part due to Dr. Thomas Holmes. I visited his unadorned mausoleum built into a hill in Brooklyn's Cypress Hills Cemetery, its door long ago sealed up. In front of it is a bench with a historic plaque installed in 2014 by historian Andrew Carroll stating that Holmes "is the man who made embalming a common practice in America" but notes that the doctor "purportedly requested that he, himself, not be embalmed."[8]

The Brooklyn-born Holmes did not invent embalming, but, as Carroll notes, he was pivotal in making it as much a part of the American grave as the casket or the tiny flags on Veteran's Day. Just as pandemics and urban development have changed the grave, war has also altered it. When soldiers died in droves far from home in the American Civil War, embalming allowed the grave to wait.

French chemist Jean-Nicolas Gannal pioneered the preservation of a corpse through arterial injection of arsenic. When his book, *The History of Embalming*, was translated into English in 1840, it greatly influenced the processes in the United States.[9] Holmes, like Gorini, was initially interested in preserving cadavers to study anatomy. The outbreak of the Civil War brought these techniques to the battlefield. Although he boasted that he had personally embalmed over 4,000 men during the war (likely an exaggeration), there was one particular job that brought embalming to the attention of the North. Historian Gary Laderman related how through the 1861 funeral of Colonel Elmer Ellsworth, "embalming was thrust into the public eye."[10] Ellsworth had taken a shotgun to the chest while removing a Confederate flag from an inn in Alexandria, Virginia. Holmes meticulously embalmed the hero, one of the first high-profile Union losses. The body traveled to the White House and New York and was viewed by hordes of mourners. While embalming allowed Ellsworth to travel, it was a ways from the future cosmetic work that could make a corpse appear lifelike, with one May 27, 1861, report remarking that the "livid paleness of the features contrasted strongly with the ruddy glow of health that had always characterized the Colonel in his lifetime."[11]

As the deaths only climbed from there, Holmes and other embalmers became part of the entourage of war, setting up tents where they practiced their grim but increasingly in-demand trade. Some saw their profiting from the bloodshed as grotesque (Holmes by several accounts charged $100 a corpse[12]), but for many, it was a solace to receive the body of their loved one and not wonder what became of them.

Physician Oliver Wendell Holmes, who traveled to the battlefield of Antietam in Maryland to find his wounded son, observed that the "slain of higher condition, 'embalmed' and iron-cased, were sliding off on the railways to their far homes; the dead of the rank-and-file were being gathered up and committed hastily to the earth."[13] It was still a luxury to bring back the dead, reserved for those who could afford it or would give up everything for this final grace. And for the first time in the country's history, the reality of a battlefield was plainly visible. In October 1862, the Manhattan gallery of Matthew Brady displayed photographs taken by Alexander Gardner.[14] They captured the aftermath of Antietam from over 250 miles away, where an estimated 22,000 were killed, wounded, or missing—the deadliest engagement in the deadliest war in American history that had occurred only weeks before, on September 17. Bodies, indistinguishable as Union or Confederate, were heaped on the grass. They were not the newspaper woodcuts that offered some visual distance or a tally of unnamed dead; they were photographs where each body could easily be perceived as an individual, and there they were without family to wash the blood from their skin or friends to build a coffin and place them within the earth. Gardner wrote of these images: "Let them aid in preventing such another calamity falling upon the nation."[15] Of course, they didn't, and if anything, Americans have only seen less of the human cost of war. From 1991 to 2009, a military policy barred media from photographing the coffins of soldiers, obscuring the losses from the wars in Iraq and Afghanistan.[16]

An even bigger funeral than Ellsworth's brought national attention to embalming, which would be bolstered by innovations like the late 19th-century commercial production of formaldehyde.[17] After Abraham Lincoln was assassinated in 1865, he was embalmed by Harry P. Cattell of Brown and Alexander, undertakers who had embalmed Lincoln's young son Willie a few years earlier.[18] His body traveled from Washington, DC, to Springfield, Illinois. The funeral train reached seven states; thousands witnessed his body.[19] The results were intermittently noted for their imperfections—an April 24, 1865, report on the body's arrival in New York City observed "the face somewhat discolored and sallow"—but overwhelmingly there was awe to see the president's body days or weeks after he had died [20].

No longer did people have to rush to host a wake and a funeral before the body on its cooling board became too unpleasant to keep at home, even when masked by mountains of lilies. Viewings could last for days, and the sendoffs could be more decadent. Embalming also contributed to the professionalization of death. It was a specialized technique, unlike keeping a body cool or digging a grave in the earth that anyone with the will could manage. Knowledge that was once part of domestic life, like the washing and care of the corpse, soon faded. In the centuries prior, death itself was not usually a business; the shroud was homemade, the carpenter who crafted the coffin also built cabinets and chairs, the sexton at the cemetery was not a full-time undertaker. By the late 19th century, the funeral industry had emerged.

Embalming also came with a perk for anyone who may have been spooked reading stories like Edgar Allan Poe's 1844 "The Premature Burial": you weren't likely to be buried alive. As grimly noted in the 1896 *Premature Burial and How It May Be Prevented,* "it is better to be killed outright by the embalmer's poisonous injections . . . than to recover underground."[21] While actual cases of it happening are incredibly rare, in the 19th century, there was a fever pitch of taphophobia or the fear of being buried alive. Societies, like the London Association for the Prevention of Premature Burial in 1896, were formed to get the word out about this supposed crisis. Safety coffins were designed so that people could escape if the worst happened, and some graves had speaking tubes so an unfortunate person could scream out for help. Along with Poe's vivid imagining of the "unendurable oppression of the lungs—the stifling fumes from the damp earth—the clinging to the death garments," sensationalist newspaper articles printed ghastly details of bodies found with signs of distress.[22] (Corpses do move around when decomposing.) One 1884 anecdote told of an unnamed woman in Wheeling, West Virginia. When she was disinterred to be moved into the family lot, the grave digger discovered her body twisted down and "the hands filled with long tufts of hair torn from the head, and the face, neck, and bosom deeply scratched and scarred, while the lining of the coffin had been torn into fragments in the desperate efforts of the entombed victim to escape from her terrible fate."[23]

Determining death has long been a place of uncertainty. Victims of the 1722 plague in Marseilles, France, were found with evidence of the bronze pins poked under their toenails to be sure they were dead.[24] There is still some debate over when a person is deceased, with the widely accepted brain death raising questions over just how much of a brain is no longer functioning for death to be declared.[25] Embalming assured you would die by being pumped full of chemicals, a dreadful idea, but perhaps better than awakening to the sound of dirt being dumped on your coffin and the sickening darkness consuming you.

Embalming was further presented as a more hygienic way of caring for the corpse, which continues to shape the public perception of natural burial, including concerns about the bodies contaminating water supplies. Notably, outcries have often come out against Muslim burial grounds in the United States, while other natural burial sites have rarely faced the same scrutiny. A traditional Muslim funeral does not include embalming, with the dead interred simply, usually in a shroud or a plain wooden coffin. Even in places that have large immigrant communities, such as New York City, there are few Muslim cemeteries, and efforts to establish them are regularly met with resistance.[26] When local governments use zoning laws to stop their construction, they often raise issues of health, such as in Walpole, Massachusetts, where one resident told a local news station in 2015 that without embalming, "all the blood, any diseases, leftover medications are still in the body and could contaminate the water supply."[27] In October 2021, Stafford County in Virginia finally gave a Muslim group permission for a cemetery following a religious discrimination lawsuit from the Justice Department after it passed an ordinance that would stop it, with concerns over water quality also being raised.[28] Sometimes these are joined by blatant Islamophobia; the city of Farmersville, Texas, was charged with violating the Religious Land Use and Institutionalized Persons Act of 2000 when in 2017 it denied an application for a Muslim cemetery. Besides concerns about health, a resident stated, "I do not want my child indoctrinated toward their religion."[29] In Dudley, Massachusetts, a Muslim cemetery received a permit in 2017 after over a year of lawsuits and a similar outcry that linked the lack of embalming to contamination of the groundwater, all with the Islamic Society of Greater Worcester only planning to bury around 15 people a year.[30,31]

While some green burial sites are welcome, others repeatedly are not, and this association from the early days of American embalming with hygiene continues to be used to discriminate in death.

Embalming is not required for burial in any state, but it is often offered as standard. It also came alongside a whole industry of objects promising to protect the body from the earth. There was a shift in language from "coffin" to "casket," a word for an object holding something treasured, as it became a new commodity and funeral centerpiece. At the National Museum of Funeral History in Houston—where exhibitions on papal funerals share space with decked out Japanese hearses and Ghanaian coffins in the shapes of chickens and cows—is a glass casket made by the DeCamp Consolidated Glass Casket Company in Oklahoma in 1925. A November 9, 1916, advertisement in the *Oklahoma City Times* that encouraged readers to buy stock in a glass casket company boasted that it will "last in the earth forever, and will not permit our loved ones to lie in a pond of water."[32] However, manufacturing glass plates big enough for a casket was incredibly difficult, and few survive. One at the Corning Museum of Glass weighs between 400 and 500 pounds.[33]

The cast iron Fisk mummy case was a decay-resistant design that went into production ahead of the widespread availability of embalming. As the New York-based Almond Dunbar Fisk wrote in his 1848 patent, he made it "to prevent the decay of the contained body."[34] Details such as thistles, roses, acorns, oak leaves, and angels decorated the metal; its shape resembled a shrouded corpse. It was pricey and was mainly favored by the wealthy who wanted to go out like Industrial Age pharaohs, with its most famed interments including Dolley Madison and President Zachary Taylor.[35]

Yet a hermetically sealed coffin and embalming cannot arrest the natural processes of corruption. After the heart stops, the body begins autolysis, or self-digestion, where the flesh eats itself with enzymes. Ancient Egyptians removed the internal organs; modern funeral directors do not, which is why many caskets have plastic linings or are covered with plastic protectors to keep the unpleasant smell and fluids from seeping out. It is not unheard of for a casket to explode if the gases from decomposition have nowhere to go.[36]

Critiques of embalming and funeral expenses have been well chronicled, including in Jessica Mitford's watershed *The American Way of Death* (1963). Still, green burial will never be for everyone, and embalming for many is not about preserving the corpse but respecting the dead. The Dover Port Mortuary in Delaware has carefully cared for the remains of thousands of American service members with meticulous embalming and tissue reconstruction, even if a closed casket funeral is planned.[37] Embalming for Black Americans, too, has long been important as a final show of respect and love for the departed. And with greener embalming practices over the years—arsenic has not been used since the early 1900s—there are ways to reduce its ecological impact.[38] Just as green burial allows some people to have their most authentic funeral, embalming offers that for others.

8 NEW IDEAS FOR THE AFTERLIFE

Just a fragment of Manhattan's First Shearith Israel Graveyard survives. Eminent domain and street widening reduced and shaved land from this rare survivor from 17th-century New York. It is elevated above the sidewalk and on most days it's only possible to glimpse it through a fence where, despite the similar shape of the old headstones to those in the colonial churchyards further downtown, the Hebrew inscriptions and symbols like Cohanim hands raised in blessing speak to its history as one of the country's earliest Jewish cemeteries.

As the COVID-19 pandemic has come in its waves through New York City, I have often thought of a headstone here for Walter Judah, who died in 1798. It is carved with a detailed view of the city as seen from the water, and from the sky emerges an arm cutting a branch from a tree with a sword. The inscription below remembers that Judah, a young medical student, died while working during a yellow fever epidemic; the stone reads, "the good that he did was the cause of his death."[1] Many wealthy and middle-class people fled during these outbreaks—as they did in spring 2020 from COVID-19—but Judah remained. If not for this tombstone, his sacrifice may have been forgotten.

There are few public memorials to the losses from disease. Those that exist, like the New York City AIDS Memorial opened in 2016, rarely list the individual dead. Cemeteries are where we can remember the people who died, and those who gave their lives to the care of others.

Even during a pandemic, the grave maintains a strange invisibility. In April 2020, I went to Green-Wood for a walk and was startled by the disconnect between people strolling and taking conference calls while in the same place the crematorium was working overtime into the night. At a moment of mass death, it was possible to look away. Still, many had to plan funerals, attend Zoom memorials, and grapple with the limited disposition options. With all of the developments in society and technology over the past decades, the innovations in the grave have been minimal, although that may be changing.

"2020 made death and funeral arrangements a lot more primary for a lot of people, and it definitely changed the tenor of how people come to us," said Anna Swenson, the Outreach Manager at Recompose in Seattle, Washington.

Recompose is offering something radically new. The company uses what's known as natural organic reduction (NOR), frequently referred to as human composting, which is based on the longstanding process of livestock composting. Within their facility's vessels, bodies become nutrient-rich soil. I started following their work in 2015 when founder Katrina Spade was fundraising on Kickstarter for an alternative to burial and cremation that would allow the body to be part of a natural ecosystem.

"When you choose Recompose, you don't really have a grave," Swenson said. "Katrina has been really clear that she doesn't want people buying specific trees or memorial benches. She wants it to be more of the idea of returning to the collective and getting people to break out of this idea of individualism. It opens up a lot of opportunities to ask, 'what is the purpose of a grave? Is it to honor the person and remember the person, and what other ways can we do that?'"

NOR was legalized for use on human remains in Washington in 2019.[2] The first bodies entered the Recompose NOR vessels on December 20, 2020. The facility opened with ten vessels, each a steel cylinder within a large hexagonal frame that resembles a giant beehive, and it has been operating at capacity in the months since. This facility in Kent, Washington, is the first of its kind and has its own ceremonies of death, beginning with the "laying in"—an inverse of the "laying out" for conventional burial—of a body in the vessel, which is filled with a mix of wood chips, alfalfa, and straw. After about 30 days of careful monitoring of the temperature, moisture, oxygen, and nitrogen to ensure the bacteria can do their decomposition work while the vessels slowly rotate, their staff removes the fresh soil for aeration in a curing bin. The result is something like the topsoil you might buy at a nursery. Recompose states that each body creates one cubic yard of nutrient-rich soil that can be placed where it is needed or somewhere meaningful.[3] Swenson said that one of their first people was Northern California organic farming pioneer Amigo Bob Cantisano. The soil from his body was used on the land that he stewarded for decades and delivered in small portions to other farms, with some friends using it to inoculate their compost piles.

Soil from the bodies processed at Recompose can be donated to an ecological restoration project at Bells Mountain, a 700-acre nonprofit land trust in southern Washington. After honoring what these people are giving back, they are put in the ground together and put to work, such as in restoring an area overtaken by invasive Himalayan blackberries. There are no plaques on trees here, no markers on the ground. It challenges people to rethink the grave beyond cremation or green burial. The memorial is the land itself. Perhaps if the utilitarian Jeremy Bentham were alive in Seattle in 2022, he would choose to be composted. Instead of shocking his friends with his glass eyes for his auto-icon, he might carry a pocketful of compost. He would look forward to being able to truly transform and be of service to the woods.

A few bodies at a time in a human composting funeral home may not tip the scale, but cremation started with a handful of facilities before becoming mainstream. There are plans for another Recompose location in Seattle and a future one in Denver, Colorado, where a bill legalizing NOR in the state was signed into law in 2021.[4] Oregon also signed a similar bill into law that year, and more bills are being considered in other states. They have met some opposition, including from the Catholic Church, which stated it is a disrespectful way to treat the body. Conversely, Catholic cemeteries have been leaders in setting aside areas for green burial, with their emphases on the natural cycle of life and death and Jesus's simple, albeit brief, burial in a shroud as a model.[5] New York State Catholic Conference's objection states that the process is "more appropriate for vegetable trimmings and eggshells than for human bodies," suggesting there may be a branding issue in "human composting."[6]

Besides promoting a new vision for the grave, Recompose as a funeral home is also very transparent about what they do and their pricing. Swenson mentioned that many people coming to them "have baggage from sometimes decades ago from having worked with a funeral home where they felt like they didn't have a choice."

The business of the grave remains very analog. The Federal Trade Commission's Funeral Rule predates the internet and only requires sharing prices over the phone or in person.[7] A 2018 survey from the Funeral Consumers Alliance and the Consumer Federation of America found that of 211 funeral homes in 25 cities, 193 had websites, and only 27 percent posted any prices online.[8] An informal survey I conducted on the ten funeral homes closest to my apartment in Brooklyn revealed seven with websites, one because it was in the Service Corporation International conglomerate of mortuary chains. I could not find pricing on any of them, although one offered me a free casket "*with certain packages" in a pop-up ad. Another stated in its payment options that its staff would help me start a crowdfunding campaign for the cost of its services, which went undisclosed.

It is unquestionably delicate to talk about how much it will cost to bury or cremate someone, and if you want a funeral with the casket, viewing, services, flowers, freshly waxed hearse, and a conventional grave, it will, of course, not be cheap—but it's a price many are willing to pay to give their loved one a send-off fitting to their memory. (According to the National Funeral Directors Association, the national median cost of a funeral with a viewing and burial in 2021 was $7,848. Cremation only made a slight difference at $6,971.[9]) If I were trying to care for someone immediately at the funeral homes in my neighborhood, calling each for quotes in a time of grief would be exhausting.

Some startups are offering cremations that can be totally booked online—from the body pickup to the return of the ashes—with a flat quote, although their availability is limited. As a 2022 *New York Times* story on these companies noted, many states require funeral homes to have facilities like large display rooms and viewing areas, making these direct-to-consumer options impossible or more difficult to establish.[10]

There are other efforts to bring the grave itself online. With more and more of our lives lived virtually, those avatars of ourselves—our Twitter feeds, our Instagram accounts, our trails of messages across untold platforms—are a major part of what we leave behind. Mourning today is as likely to occur in the comment section on a final Instagram post as at a headstone. In 1995, Canadian internet pioneer Mike Kibbee started the World Wide Cemetery with a onetime fee for a "permanent memorial."[11] He was then in his early 30s and dying of Hodgkin's lymphoma, and as his own March 8, 1997, obituary states on the site, he made "death a project," including building his own coffin of pine.[12] These types of online memorials have continued to expand alongside digital communities, such as in massively multiplayer online (MMO) gaming. In April 2020, players of *Final Fantasy XIV* staged an hour-long funeral march in the game for a player who died of COVID-19.[13] After actor Robin Williams, a passionate gamer, died in 2014, *World of Warcraft* paid tribute to him with an NPC that can be summoned genie-like from a lamp that overlooks an ocean.[14] For these memorials detached from the grave, it's not about where you are remembered, but how.

Yet the online world is ephemeral. (I know this well as a writer who contributed to publications now totally inaccessible only a decade later.) Unlike a gravestone, a virtual cemetery can lose its hosting, an update can scrub old content, and a browser can no longer support a flash plugin. Social media sites fade out of favor. And then there's the question of how authentically you can be remembered online: Appalachian bootlegger and moonshiner Marvin "Popcorn" Sutton picked his grave marker and coffin before his death in 2009, but on FindaGrave.com the epitaph he chose for his footstone—"Popcorn Said Fuck You"—is censored.[15]

Others have experimented with artificial intelligence (AI) to keep the dead present. AI specialist Eugenia Kuyda created a chatbot of her friend Roman Mazurenko who died suddenly in 2015. It was sourced from thousands of his messages collected from family and friends, with a neural network that learned how to have a dialogue based on these memories.[16] Now, anyone can download the Roman chatbot to have a conversation with him about anything. I asked this digital avatar, "Is this a grave?" He responded simply: "Yes."

Martine Rothblatt, CEO of biotech firm United Therapeutics and founder of SiriusXM radio, has been working for years on a more complex "mind clone" of her wife, Bina Aspen. BINA48—or Breakthrough Intelligence via Neural Architecture 48—is just a head and shoulders so far, but contains hundreds of hours of Bina's memories, thoughts, and beliefs.[17] Neither this, the chatbot, nor the online headstone will likely allow us to be present forever as our whole selves, but they are bringing something of a person forward through time in a way that's not dissimilar from an epitaph on a grave. The other technologies attempting this longevity, like cryopreservation and the hope for robotic bodies, are also still a distance from eternal life.

While these are new forms of memorial, they do not involve the physical grave, which has only gradually incorporated digital technology. This tends to be surface-level interventions, such as QR codes on headstones, although they do make a person's life an active element of the grave. For example, Hollywood Forever Cemetery in Los Angeles has a LifeStory Archive where videos, photos, oral stories, and other memories are preserved digitally and can be accessed in the cemetery and online.

More radical ideas have been explored but not widely implemented, such as the "transgenic tombstones" designed by Shiho Fukuhara and Georg Tremmel. Taking skin cells from a person and extracting their DNA, this genetic material is injected into a tree cell. The resulting tree would have the person's DNA in each cell, growing into a memorial.[18]

While these remain conceptual projects, they encourage a reimagining of what a 21st-century grave could be. "There are all kinds of different solutions," John Troyer, the Director of the Centre for Death and Society at the University of Bath, told me. "One is, how do we adapt and adopt new kinds of technology that augment what's already been used? I don't think it's a question of replacement. It's more a situation of just adding onto." That question, too, of how to make a new grave is something we have more opportunities for than in the past. "We are living so much longer now," Troyer said. "We have all this time to think about these things now where we didn't before."

This idea of an adding-onto—much like cremation and green burial have become parts of cemeteries—was explored in an initiative at the Centre for Death and Society. The winning design in their 2016 Future Cemetery design competition was from the DeathLAB in the Graduate School of Architecture, Planning and Preservation (GSAPP) at New

York's Columbia University and LATENT Productions. Called Sylvan Constellation, the project proposes a memorial space elevated above Bristol's Arnos Vale Cemetery. In it, decomposing biomass—the corpse's chemical and biological components—powers lights through the chemical reactions of decomposition, each waning illumination representing an individual life.[19] DeathLAB's "Constellation Park" similarly envisions glowing biomass lights suspended from the Manhattan Bridge, letting the dead be part of the city once more before their final light extinguishes.

"DeathLAB is seeking to augment the death industry to better support individual and collective needs around death, mourning, and remembrance," said architect Karla Rothstein, the Design Director at LATENT who founded DeathLAB in 2013. "What happens to a body after death is not only a question of emotional or religious convictions of individuals and communities, but touches on questions of humanity, law, spatial engineering, environmental concerns, and economic and racial equity."

She added that DeathLAB has initiated a spinoff company called AfterLight which is pursuing the eventual commercialization of a reusable memorial vessel system. Students in its graduate design and research studios have traveled across the world to understand funerary rituals and customs to inform their work which considers urban funerary infrastructure and its ecological consequences. Another project called WPA 2.0 proposes a tower of vessels that would be located in a contaminated brownfield site and could use the processing of remains as a form of bioremediation.[20]

"It is increasingly rare that urban dwellers can be memorialized within the cities that they love, proximate to their communities and the people who will mourn them," Rothstein said. "Modern origins of urban planning and civic design in North America have rarely devised long-term plans for the integration of the interment of the dead as part of civic affairs, although death and dying are a fundamental part of social and intimate life. While the experience of loss manifests in the most individual of ways, as specific and personal as the relationships we have with our loved ones, mourning is a shared human experience, an opportunity to care for ourselves, and strengthen our communal ties and shared purposes."

These ideas may seem futuristic, but they can compel us to ask why we don't have more meaningful, modern memorials for the departed in public spaces that don't solely have to do with tragedy or war. To remember an ordinary loved one visibly in a city where they lived is powerful, and moving that outside of the confines of the cemetery extends their memory. The rise of cremation, green burial, and now human composting have added more choice to the grave. However, there is still room to make this final statement more purposeful, sustainable, and accessible.

To assure these new approaches are widely available to the public will take more change in our funerary systems and visibility. It is notable that a few public figures have recently had alternative choices for their graves. After Desmond Tutu died on December 26, 2021, he was interred in a plain pine coffin adorned with a small bouquet of white carnations. Rather than be buried, his body underwent aquamation, also known as alkaline hydrolysis or water cremation.[21] It has been approved in a few states and uses water and alkaline chemicals combined with heat to accelerate decomposition in a six- to eight-hour-long process. When actor Luke Perry died on March 4, 2019, he was buried in a "mushroom suit" developed by Jae Rhim Lee of the Coeio green burial company in California.[22] The biodegradable cotton burial suit is made with mushrooms and microorganisms intended to grow and neutralize the cadaver's toxins. Each of these examples is just one person choosing something different, but they foster a wider conversation about what could be possible for the grave.

9 DEAD SPACE

New ideas emerging for the grave attempt to alleviate land use and create more sustainable deathways, yet there's still the question of the future for existing graves in the United States. They sprawl alongside highways, are wedged into neighborhoods that grew up around them, and have often outlasted the communities, churches, or families that established them. Some cemeteries are reaching capacity, meaning their longtime source of income—selling lots—may vanish. Only a few have large endowments or crematoria that can provide ongoing revenue. And with older cemeteries becoming increasingly crowded, the greenspace that made them such a breath of fresh air in the 19th century can be lost in a cluttered stoneyard.

For cemeteries that reach the culmination of their time as active burial grounds, there are other pathways for reimagining themselves as spaces for the living rather than becoming static echoes of the past.

Annual interments at the Woodlands in Philadelphia are down to only a handful each year, and the sales of plots no longer fund operations. Instead, the cemetery focuses on being a haven for its neighborhood, welcoming activities that many American burial grounds do not. Jessica Baumert, Executive Director of the Woodlands, told me that this is in keeping with their founding, with the 1840 Articles of Incorporation stating the cemetery would provide burial space to ease overcrowding and "health and solace to the living."[1] On its 54 acres in a dense urban area, dogs can be walked, picnics are welcome, and biking is permitted on the roads. Joggers loop around its graves on a perimeter path, and volunteers plant flowers in the historic cradle graves through an incredibly successful program called the Grave Gardeners.

The cradle grave was fashionable in the 19th century; its name comes from its shape where a marble or granite headstone and footstone are connected by two walls, leaving the ground open in the center. Loved ones were intended to plant gardens in this space, but as people moved away and families died off or stopped visiting, the cradle graves became barren or overgrown with weeds.

After Baumert joined the Woodlands, she happened on an old Philadelphia guidebook that noted the "French-style" cradle graves at the cemetery, which were "further enhanced by the profusion of roses and other choice flowers."[2] The roses were long gone, but many of the cradle graves remained. In 2016, the Grave Gardeners program was launched, and demand has increased each year. Baumert said that many of the 2022 applicants had discovered the Woodlands during the COVD-19 pandemic as an outdoor respite. A number of them wanted to garden in memory of someone they had lost. As cemetery graves have become more infrequent with the rise of cremation, and as regulations have commonly limited graveside plantings, being able to create a living memorial for a person in a place of mourning is rare.

"There's still that need to have a place you can go to that helps you remember someone, whether that person's buried there or not," Baumert said. "I think a cemetery can fill that role much better than your typical park because it's a more reflective space. There's an opportunity [for it] to become really meaningful for people who don't have loved ones buried there."

The land that became the Woodlands was previously a garden estate where in the late 18th-century amateur botanist William Hamilton cultivated specimens from across the globe, including some of the country's earliest ginkgoes and flora collected by explorers Lewis and Clark. Now, the gardening involves over 135 volunteers who mostly do not have a family connection to the cemetery. Learning about the cemetery's history is part of the program, along with an overview of gardening basics so anyone can feel confident in working the earth. The plantings are based on what would have been present in late 19th-century Philadelphia, from the muted colors of Lenten roses that bloom in winter to the bright daffodils and tulips of spring, to the kaleidoscopic summer hues of red poppies, snapdragons, foxglove, cornflowers, and white columbines.

The gardeners research the graves they are tending, with one recently throwing a birthday party for the person under their cradle grave. Just as in the 19th century it was not uncommon to have a picnic in a cemetery or go for a carriage ride, that same sense of community is being instilled, but through care for strangers. Even on an autumn visit I made in 2018, the cradle graves were flourishing; ivy, ferns, and other greenery spilled over the marble monuments in a cascade. The plantings added to rather than detracted from the old graves, the visible attention a tribute to those buried and the people who use the space today.

Other historic cemeteries are anticipating climate change and evaluating how the landscape that was so much a part of the cemetery's founding can be carried forward with new meaning. In January 2022, I talked with Joe Charap, the Director of Horticulture at Brooklyn's Green-Wood, outside a cemetery outbuilding. Through a window, I could see a corpse flower in its leaf state, one of his horticultural experiments alongside the greater work of thoughtfully nurturing a landscape with 150 years of history.

"Green-Wood and other green spaces have the potential to serve as places for advocacy, for the preservation of green spaces writ large in urban environments," Charap said. "They can do that by limiting their negative impacts on the environment through their operations." One idea is to shift away from the pristine green lawn popular across the country in cemeteries and front yards. A hill near the chapel was transformed into a meadow filled with biodiverse plants that draw pollinators throughout the seasons. In other sections of the cemetery, the grass has been allowed to grow long in the summer as part of a partnership with Cornell University to examine alternatives to turf grass for a climate-resilient landscape.[3] Just as cemeteries set a model for parks in the 19th century, they can now set new trends in urban nature.

"We are preserving this landscape in perpetuity for our lot owners and for the loved ones that are buried here, and there's no reason at the same time why it can't serve the people that are around us," Charap said. While the cemetery opened as an island of mourning, neighborhoods with diverse needs now surround it. He discussed how there is a responsibility to take on activities related to stewardship that may not have any short-term benefits, such as stormwater mediation to ease their influence on the combined sewer overflows in the area. Trees have been planted on the cemetery's perimeter and street tree workshops have been organized to share knowledge of caring for nature in a city.

Cemetery programs to support maintenance and conservation have similarly embraced this role as community greenspace. The Congressional Cemetery in Washington, DC, which dates to 1807, has an active members-only dog walking program. By contributing a quarter of the cemetery's operating costs, the dog walkers have helped with preservation and added a vitality to a once desolate and overgrown place.[4] There is almost always someone there from dawn to dusk walking a dog, contrasting to many old cemeteries that can be completely empty, even on a beautiful afternoon.

The grave can also be an educational resource. In 2015, the World Monuments Fund launched a pilot program for the Bridge to Crafts Careers initiative to train a new generation in stone conservation. Aimed at underrepresented youth who live in New York City, the program offers hands-on experience and training with masonry, conservation, and maintenance at Woodlawn in the Bronx.[5] A cemetery is ideal for this learning, with its range of monuments in marble, slate, granite, sandstone, and other materials. The program has since expanded to Green-Wood and the African American Cemetery in Rye, New York.

"I think, on the one hand, cemeteries are extremely timeless, but on the other hand, you can still see the hand of time here," said Neela Wickremesinghe, the Director of Restoration and Preservation at Green-Wood who also works with Bridge to Crafts Careers. Green-Wood is one of the few cemeteries with a full-time restoration department for work that she describes as "never-ending," whether it's resetting monuments or stonework repairs. I visited Wickremesinghe in the cemetery workshop where she and her team engage in conservation that can range from a colonial-era headstone where the dates have almost entirely flaked off to elements of a larger mausoleum. As she explained, the goal, like in most art conservation, is to only do things that could be undone in the future.

She noted that there used to be a stronger link between decorative arts, architecture, and monuments, and while there aren't as many stone carvers as there once were, it does not mean it is an obsolete profession. A cemetery can be a leader in fostering these careers, although there's an added weight that's different from working in other settings.

"I often think about folks here whose name might only be in three places," Wickremesinghe said. "Our chronology book, our lot book, and on their headstone, if they have one. So it makes it that much more important."

In the past decade, several cemeteries have experimented with the possibilities for historic graves as places of celebration, community, and joy. From 2013 to 2015, I collaborated on a series of events at Green-Wood that aimed to bring people into the cemetery in a new way. Working with Green-Wood's Manager of Programs Chelsea Dowell, my colleague Megan Roberts spearheaded these events for the travel site *Atlas Obscura*, where I was then the senior editor. The gatherings we worked on ranged from an intimate nighttime symbolism walk that concluded in a candlelit mausoleum with cryptic symbols carved on its tombs to larger celebrations in the catacombs, a tunnel-like group mausoleum. There were bars tucked away beneath weeping beech trees laced with fairy lights and musicians playing music on the winding paths.

"To me, those events were always meant to be a love song to the cemetery," Megan told me in a conversation where we looked back at these events. "It was important to me that they would open people's eyes about what cemeteries could be and rethink our relationship with burial spaces. I was always hoping it would not be a one-off experience, but it would make people want to come back and explore more and learn about the space by daylight."

We always tried to put these events in dialogue with the individuals buried there rather than use the site as a backdrop, with the catacombs event acting as a tribute to the Gilded Age tastemaker Ward McAllister who was interred within. One person buried at Green-Wood—19th-century entertainment impresario William Niblo—is said to have had decadent parties at his mausoleum before his death. Megan said one of her favorites was at the grave of Charlotte Canda, whose tomb is a beautiful white marble confection of spires and carved roses, stars, and butterflies, all centered on a statue of Canda herself as she looked on the night of her 17th birthday when she died in a carriage accident. A dancer with the Carte Blanche Performance group wore an elaborate paper gown, and people were invited to slowly dance with her and write messages to deceased loved ones on the dress.

We heard from people having magical life moments at these events, like getting engaged, and from those experiencing grief who found release.

"Something that a lot of people who don't spend time in cemeteries don't realize is they are these true retreats from the hustle and bustle of the city," Megan said. "Just being in Green-Wood on a warm summer night there are fireflies. In Laurel Hill in Philadelphia, we had a night where we had a theremin player and a family of foxes that live in the cemetery came out to watch the performance."

One night that stands out to me is being by one of Green-Wood's glacial ponds after a hectic day of setting up for an evening of performances and having a moment to sit and listen as an accordion player drifted in a rowboat on the water. I thought of all the people buried here and how they wanted to be part of this landscape where, from its start, the goal was to have a different relationship with death. Although I do not believe that a cemetery can just be a venue, I do think there are ways to bring people in to care not only for major historic sites like Green-Wood, but any cemetery. Even a suburban cemetery with little romantic landscaping can offer stargazing nights, and a neighborhood churchyard can invite an artist to respond to the site—opportunities to meditate on what these places can mean.

Some cemeteries have hosted art installations that raise awareness for graves that have been overlooked. I spoke with Richard Parker, the Executive Director of the Historic Oakland Foundation in Atlanta, Georgia. Like the Woodlands, Oakland Cemetery is exceptionally open for visitors in terms of what is welcome, including picnics, dog walking, biking, and jogging. They also regularly have artists create site-specific works.

"Oakland, for many people, is their neighborhood park, so we think of our approach to the public as expansive and welcoming rather than exclusionary," Parker said. "We try to be inclusive of all and find new ways to reach new people and provide a critical resource for them."

Oakland is surrounded by neighborhoods in the center of the city. From its beginnings in 1850, it was popular for Sunday carriage rides and picnics. It continues to be an urban retreat and is the city's third-largest greenspace with gardens of daffodils in spring and irises in summer.[6] Oak trees shade the grounds.

The most noticeable and tallest monument is for a Confederate burial ground. Recent artwork has raised visibility for areas of the cemetery that are less visible, particularly the African American burial ground, where markers made of wood or objects like shells have disappeared over time. The 2021 edition of Arts at Oakland featured *Invisible Flock* by Atlanta visual artists Zipporah Camille Thompson and Dorothy O'Connor. The exhibit was a flock of birds made of varying wood veneers with patterns reminiscent of African American freedom quilting. Every bird contained a vessel with burial materials and the name of someone interred in the grounds. In their beaks, flagging tape formed into a flower or leaf represented the surveying work done to recover the locations of over 870 graves.[7] Also in 2021, Atlanta artist and activist Charmaine Minniefield installed a praise house at the unmarked graves.[8] The wooden structure was inspired by those used in the South by enslaved people for worship and included sound and video evoking the stories long ignored beneath the ground.

"I think art is a way to reflect on the past through a contemporary lens," Parker said. "You certainly can do that through other mediums, but art is particularly effective. It can ask, 'what does Oakland mean as a place?' And what does it mean to how we think about death? How we think about life? How we think about our city, our city's history, and where we are in the current political moment? We are trying to change the definition of what a cemetery should be."

These installations are temporary, but other artists are considering the eternal potential of a historic cemetery. In Woodlawn, at the base of a small slope, is a larger-than-life bronze sculpture of two nude women holding each other in bed. Their hair is splayed across a shared pillow, and a sheet tangles over their legs like classical drapery, their toes just barely touching. Artist Patricia Cronin installed a Carrara marble work in 2002 before replacing it with the bronze version in 2011.[9] Called *Memorial to a Marriage*, it is for the plot where she and her wife, fellow artist Deborah Kass, will someday be buried and was a tribute to the marriage they thought they would never have.

"It was the only official thing I could come up with, besides a will or a health care proxy, or boring, depressing documents," she told me during a January 2022 visit to her Brooklyn studio. She explained that since all they could legally obtain to show their partnership was related to death and dying, she decided to respond to these limitations by creating art in a cemetery.

Inspired by the ancient Roman sculpture *Sleeping Hermaphroditus*, the work also echoes 19th-century funerary art such as William Henry Rinehart's *Sleeping Children* who have a similar drapery at their hips and a shared pillow, as well as Gustave Courbet's 1866 *The Sleepers* of two women entwined.

"I feel like I snuck in, in a way only an artist could," she told me, referring to the fact that the sculpture is among the large mausoleums and monuments showcasing the male-dominated wealth of the Gilded Age. Now, 20 years following that initial installation, we talked about how although same-sex marriage has been legal in the United States since 2013, the work is a reminder of the places where it remains illegal and even punishable by death. It is still the only Marriage Equality monument in the world.[10]

"I didn't know the Defense of Marriage Act was going to be overturned so quickly; I didn't know gay marriage was going to be legal," she said. "I thought I was making this for an audience that didn't exist yet. I thought maybe someone who wasn't born yet will walk through Woodlawn and they'll go, 'Oh my goodness, can you believe that in the United States it used to be illegal to have [a] same-sex marriage?'"

The exhibition date of *Memorial to a Marriage* is November 3, 2002 to Eternity. Amid the monuments to New York's titans of industry is this lesbian couple in a peaceful sleep.

"If it's between ephemeral and permanence, I'm always going to vote for the permanence," she said. "Even if that doesn't last forever. You know, what is eternity? But as long as there's a Woodlawn, the sculpture will be there."

The sculpture is in what feels like a sunken garden. You gaze down at it, whereas other monuments demand you look up. I've seen it across seasons. In autumn, leaves fall into the drapery's metal folds and in the crooks of the sculpted limbs; in winter, it can be lost beneath the snow. When it rains, water pools in the space between where their toes touch. It may eventually wear down and become shiny from the hands of those who visit. Maybe long after Cronin and Kass and all of us on the planet at this moment are in the ground or ashes or compost in a field, someone can bend down to touch the bronze and remember why it was put here.

We never know how far the grave is from us. As I write this, I am 36 years old, soon to turn 37. The grave for me is something I can still write about abstractly, but the truth is I can never really know. In the first chapter of this book, I wrote that I had asked in my final wishes to be cremated and have my ashes scattered, but after talking to people working in different aspects of the grave, I'm not sure that's still what I want. It is what I chose because it was the easiest. I have thought about how meaningful it would be to have soil composted from my body laid on the ground in my local park, where I walk almost every morning. I have envisioned my ashes being turned into a diamond to pass down as an heirloom. I have considered how I could be buried somewhere to help protect the land.

Whether within my lifetime there will be bridges illuminated with a constellation of the departed, or if earth created through the decomposition of our neighbors will help local flowers grow, the graves already in our cities will still be there. Graves are among the most enduring type of landscape. They have shaped the topography, with streets running at crooked angles to jog around their borders. They rest beneath our daily paths, and even if we don't see them, they're reminders that long before us, there were others who made choices about what this world looks like for both the living and the dead.

We may never truly shake the grave. But cemeteries cannot sprawl as they have forever until headstones cover the globe, and preserving every cemetery in perpetuity is impossible. There is room to instill new ideas into historical places while rethinking if we require them in the future. There is a need to move the grave back into our communities. I am hopeful that we can do better about respectfully and meaningfully honoring all the departed. I want to live in a good place to die.

NOTES

Chapter 1

1 Hovers, Erella, et al., "An Early Case of Color Symbolism," *Current Anthropology* 44, n. 4 (2003): 491–522.

2 Martinón-Torres, M., d'Errico, F., Santos, E. et al., "Earliest known human burial in Africa," *Nature* 593 (2021): 95–100.

3 Hertz, Robert, *Death and the Right Hand*, trans. Rodney Needham and Claudia Needham (Glencoe, Ill.: Free Press, 1960): 27.

4 Viollet-le-Duc, Eugène-Emmanuel, *Dictionnaire raisonné de l'architecture française du XIe siècle* (France: A. Morel, 1868): 21.

5 D'Imperio, Chuck, "The Most Unusual Grave in Upstate NY Has Tiny Window to Honor Boy's Final Wish," *NYup.com*, March 21, 2018, https://www.newyorkupstate.com/road-trips /2018/03/the_most_unusual_grave_in_upstate_ny_has_tiny _window_to_honor_boys_final_wish.html.

6 Fields, Liz, "Biker Buried astride Beloved Harley in Plexiglas Casket," *ABC News*, February 1, 2014, https:// abcnews.go.com/US/biker-buried-astride-beloved-harley -plexiglas-casket/story?id=22329160.

7 "Ashes to Ashes," *Skiing* magazine, January 1998.

8 Ingram, Simon, "The Living Paths of the Dead," *The Guardian*, February 8, 2016, https://www.theguardian.com/environment /2016/feb/08/lake-district-corpse-road-coffin-trail-spirit-ghost.

9 "Graves," Savannah/Hilton Head International Airport, accessed March 16, 2022, https://savannahairport.com/ business/about/graves/.

10 "Historic 'Grave in the Middle of the Road' Being Excavated in Johnson County," *Fox 59*, May 11, 2016, https://fox59 .com/news/historic-grave-in-the-middle-of-the-road-being -excavated-in-johnson-county/.

11 Applebome, Peter, "Giving Names to Souls Forgotten No Longer," *New York Times*, December 13, 2007, https://www .nytimes.com/2007/12/13/nyregion/13towns.html.

12 Brandes, Heide, "On Iconic U.S. Route 66, German and Italian POWs Lie in Oklahoma Graves," *Reuters*, June 5, 2014, https://www.reuters.com/article/us-usa-cemetery-oklahoma -idUSKBN0EG1QS20140605.

13 Lovejoy, Bess, "These Connected Graves in the Netherlands Prove Love Conquers All," *Mental Floss,* October 6, 2017, https://www.mentalfloss.com/article/505109/these-connected -graves-netherlands-prove-love-conquers-all.

14 Freeman, Lee, "The Legend of Mountain Tom Clark," *Alabama Heritage*, October 5, 2016, https://www .alabamaheritage.com/from-the-vault/-the-legend-of -mountain-tom-clark.

15 "Burying the dead," UK Parliament, accessed March 16, 2022, https://www.parliament.uk/about/living-heritage/ transformingsociety/private-lives/death-dying/dying-and -death/burying/.

16 Lynch, Michael, "Grave Problem," *Reason*, July 1, 1999, https://reason.com/1999/07/01/grave-problem/.

17 Jordan, Terry G., *Texas Graveyards: A Cultural Legacy*, (Austin, Tex.: University of Texas Press, 1982): 7.

18 Roberts, Sam, "100 Years after New York's Deadliest Subway Crash," *New York Times*, November 1, 2018, https://www.nytimes.com/2018/11/01/nyregion/100-years-after-new-yorks-deadliest-subway-crash.html.

19 Margolies, Jane, "Real Estate for the Afterlife," *New York Times*, March 15, 2019, https://www.nytimes.com/2019/03/15/realestate/real-estate-for-the-afterlife.html.

20 Roberts, Sam, "Koch, Resolved to Spend Eternity in Manhattan, Buys a Cemetery Plot," *New York Times*, April 22, 2008, https://www.nytimes.com/2008/04/22/nyregion/22koch.html.

21 Feuer, Alan, and William K. Rashbaum, "'We Ran out of Space': Bodies Pile up as N.Y. Struggles to Bury Its Dead," *New York Times*, April 30, 2020, https://www.nytimes.com/2020/04/30/nyregion/coronavirus-nyc-funeral-home-morgue-bodies.html.

22 Kravitz, Derek, "Bodies of Hundreds of New York COVID Victims Still in Trucks on Brooklyn Pier," *THE CITY*, May 6, 2021, https://www.thecity.nyc/missing-them/2021/5/6/22423844/new-york-covid-victims-still-in-trucks-on-brooklyn-pier.

Chapter 2

1 "Pinson Mounds State Archaeological Park," Tennessee Department of Environment and Conservation, accessed

February 7, 2022, https://www.tn.gov/environment/program-areas/arch-archaeology/state-archaeological-parks-areas/pinson-mounds-state-archaeological-park.html.

2 Mainfort, Robert C, et al., *Pinson Mounds: Middle Woodland Ceremonialism in the Midsouth* (Fayetteville, Ark.: University Of Arkansas Press, 2013): 117.

3 Baires, Sarah, "White Settlers Buried the Truth about the Midwest's Mysterious Mound Cities," *Smithsonian Magazine*, February 23, 2018, https://www.smithsonianmag.com/history/white-settlers-buried-truth-about-midwests-mysterious-mound-cities-180968246/.

4 "Native American Graves Protection and Repatriation Act," National Park Service, accessed March 16, 2022, https://www.nps.gov/subjects/nagpra/index.htm.

5 City of New York Office of the President of the Borough of Queens, *Description of Private and Family Cemeteries in the Borough of Queens*, compiled by Charles U. Powell, C. E., 1932.

6 "Indian Chief To Be Buried Tomorrow," *The Brooklyn Daily Eagle* (Brooklyn, New York), September 4, 1927.

7 Breitenbach, Dagmar, "R.I.P.: German Funeral Rites and Practices," *Deutsche Welle (DW)*, November 11, 2020, https://www.dw.com/en/rip-german-funeral-rites-and-practices/a-45382829.

8 Yingqi, Cheng, "Govt Buries Concerns over Cemetery Fees," *China Daily*, April 6, 2011, https://www.chinadaily.com.cn/china/2011-04/06/content_12275771.htm.

9   "Cimetière Du Père-Lachaise: Les Équipements Cinéraires,"
    Paris.fr, accessed March 16, 2022, https://www.paris.fr/pages/
    cimetiere-du-pere-lachaise-les-equipements-cineraires-17456.

10 "City of London Cemetery Will Never Run out of Space," City
    of London Newsroom, May 9, 2016, https://news.cityoflondon
    .gov.uk/city-of-london-cemetery-will-never-run-out-of
    -space/.

11 Stephenson, Wesley, "Do the Dead Outnumber the Living?,"
    BBC News, February 4, 2012, https://www.bbc.com/news/
    magazine-16870579.

12 American Society of Planning Officials, *Cemeteries in the City
    Plan*, July 1950.

13 "Flatbush Dutch Reformed Church & Expanded Site,"
    Historic Districts Council, accessed March 16, 2022, https://
    hdc.org/buildings/flatbush-dutch-reformed-church-expanded
    -site/.

14 "Flatbush Dutch Reformed Church," Historic Districts
    Council's Six to Celebrate, accessed March 16, 2022,
    https://6tocelebrate.org/site/flatbush-dutch-reformed
    -church/.

15 "The Church," The Lefferts Family Papers at Brooklyn
    Historical Society, accessed March 16, 2022. https://lefferts
    .brooklynhistory.org/the-church/.

16 H. P. Lovecraft, "The Horror at Red Hook," 1925.

17 "The Oldest Gravestone in the Trinity Churchyard," Trinity
    Church Wall Street, August 5, 2016, https://trinitywallstreet
    .org/stories-news/oldest-gravestone-trinity-churchyard.

18 Lefferts Vanderbilt, Gertrude, *The Social History of Flatbush
    and Manners and Customs of the Dutch Settlers in Kings
    County* (New York: D. Appleton and Company, 1899): 175.

19 French, Mary, "Flatbush Reformed Dutch Church Cemetery," New York City Cemetery Project, July 9, 2021, https://nycemetery.wordpress.com/2021/07/09/flatbush-reformed-dutch-church-cemetery/.

20 "Where the Color Line Exists: No Equal Rights in Some of the Cemeteries," *The Brooklyn Daily Eagle* (Brooklyn, New York), December 7, 1890.

21 "Flatbush African Burial Ground Remembrance and Redevelopment," New York City Department of Housing Preservation and Development, accessed March 16, 2022, https://www1.nyc.gov/site/hpd/services-and-information/fabg-site-history.page.

22 Obituary for Eve, *The Long-Island Star* (Brooklyn, New York), March 29, 1810.

23 "Mayor de Blasio and Council Member Eugene Announce Plans to Transform Flatbush Site into Affordable Housing," New York City Department of Housing Preservation and Development, October 9, 2020, https://www1.nyc.gov/office-of-the-mayor/news/705-20/mayor-de-blasio-council-member-eugene-plans-transform-flatbush-site-affordable.

24 Tashjian, Ann and Dickran, "The Afro-American Section of Newport, Rhode Island's Common Burying Ground," *Cemeteries and Gravemarkers: Voices of American Culture*, edited by Richard E. Meyer (Logan, Utah: Utah State University Press, 1992): 171.

25 The African Burial Ground Project, Howard University, *Skeletal Biology Final Report: Volume I*, December 2004.

26 "Site Heritage," New Museum, accessed March 16, 2022, https://www.newmuseum.org/pages/view/building-1.

27 "126th Street African Burial Ground Memorial and Mixed-Use Project," New York City Economic Development Corporation, accessed March 16, 2022, https://edc.nyc/project/east-126th-harlem-african-burial-ground-project.

28 Jones-Gorman, Jessica, "Asphalt, Shops Cover NYC Burial Ground for Slaves," *Staten Island Advance*, February 15, 2022, https://www.silive.com/news/2022/02/asphalt-shops-cover-nyc-burial-ground-for-slaves-filmmaker-haunted-by-its-history-hopes-to-inspire-change.html.

29 "Use of the Quarterly Meeting Cemetery and Information on Preparation for Death," New York Quarterly Meeting, accessed March 16, 2022, https://www.nycquakers.org/2017/06/29/use-of-the-quarterly-meeting-cemetery-and-information-on-preparation-for-death/.

30 "The Quaker Menace," Pembroke Historical Society, accessed March 16, 2022, https://www.pembrokehistoricalsociety.org/the-quaker-menace.html.

31 "NYQM Cemetery," New York Quarterly Meeting, accessed March 16, 2022, https://www.nycquakers.org/resources/cemetery/.

32 French, Mary, "The Marble Cemeteries," New York City Cemetery Project, June 12, 2014, https://nycemetery.wordpress.com/2014/06/12/the-marble-cemeteries/.

Chapter 3

1 "Hymn Sung at Consecration," Mount Auburn Cemetery, accessed March 16, 2022, https://mountauburn.org/hymn-sung-at-consecration/.

2 "Boston Courier's Account of the Consecration," Mount Auburn Cemetery, Accessed March 24, 2022, https://mountauburn.org/boston-courier-account-of-the-consecration/.

3 "History of Central Burying Ground," *Historic Burying Grounds Initiative Newsletter*, Boston Parks & Recreation Department, Fall 2021.

4 November 6, 1795, meeting of the freeholders and other inhabitants of the town, *Documents of the City of Boston* (United States: City Council, Printing Section, 1904): 412.

5 *Preservation Guidelines for Municipally Owned Historic Burial Grounds and Cemeteries*, Third Edition, Massachusetts Department of Conservation and Recreation, DCR Historic Cemeteries Preservation Initiative, 2009.

6 "Emergencies: Management of Dead Bodies," World Health Organization, December 11, 2019, https://www.who.int/news-room/questions-and-answers/item/emergencies-management-of-dead-bodies.

7 Turnbull, Samuel E., "The Subway," *National Magazine*, Volume 2 (1895).

8 "Site History," Les Catacombes de Paris, accessed March 19, 2022, https://www.catacombes.paris.fr/en/history/site-history.

9 *Mount Auburn Illustrated: In Highly Finished Line Engraving, from Drawings Taken on the Spot, by James Smillie. With Descriptive Notices by Cornelia W. Walter* (United States: Martin and Johnson, 1847), 29.

10 "Mount Auburn," *The Evening Post* (New York, New York), September 21, 1833.

11 Arfwedson, Carl David, *The United States and Canada in 1832, 1833, and 1834* (United Kingdom: R. Bentley, 1834): 211.

12 Smith, Henry Perry, *History of Oakwood Cemetery* (Syracuse, New York: H. P. Smith & Co., 1871), 36.

13 "History," Laurel Hill Cemetery, accessed March 16, 2022, https://thelaurelhillcemetery.org/about/history.

14 "Caution to Sportsmen in the Neighborhood of the Green-Wood Cemetery," *The Long-Island Star* (Brooklyn, New York), October 17, 1839.

15 Downing, Andrew Jackson, "Public Cemeteries and Public Gardens, July, 1849," *Rural Essays* (New York: George P. Putnam and Company, 1853): 157.

16 *The Liberator* (Boston, Massachusetts), May 26, 1832.

Chapter 4

1 "Most Holy Trinity Cemetery," Most Holy Trinity - St. Mary Parish, accessed March 16, 2022, https://trinity-stmary.org/history/most-holy-trinity-cemeterynbsp.

2 "Taking a Tour of Brooklyn's 'Green Oasis,'" *NPR*, June 7, 2009, https://www.npr.org/templates/story/story.php?storyId=105082304.

3 "Woodlawn Cemetery- Huntington Mausoleum," Historic Districts Council's Six to Celebrate, accessed March 16, 2022, https://6tocelebrate.org/site/huntington-mausoleum/.

4 "Jay Gould's Body at Rest," *New York Times*, December 7, 1892.

5 Hoyt, Edwin Palmer, *The Goulds: A Social History* (New York: Weybright and Talley, 1969): 128.

6 Kelly, John, "Is That a Greenhouse? No, It's a Tomb," *Washington Post*, January 12, 2013, https://www .washingtonpost.com/local/is-that-a-greenhouse-no-its-a -tomb/2013/01/12/5fd2256e-5b3c-11e2-88d0-c4cf65c3ad15 _story.html.

7 Costa, Caroline de, and Francesca Miller, "American Resurrection and the 1788 New York Doctors' Riot," *The Lancet* 377 (9762) (January 22, 2011): 292–93.

8 Wilf, Steven Robert, "Anatomy and Punishment in Late Eighteenth-Century New York," *Journal of Social History* 22, no. 3 (1989): 507–30.

9 Bain, Frederika Elizabeth, *Dismemberment in the Medieval and Early Modern English Imaginary: The Performance of Difference* (Germany: De Gruyter, 2020): 229.

10 Wells, Ali, "Rest in Pieces: The Story of a Hanged Woman and Her Journey to Becoming a Museum Object," The Power of the Criminal Corpse: University of Leicester (blog), July 27, 2016, https://staffblogs.le.ac.uk/crimcorpse/2016/07/27/rest -in-pieces/.

11 "Pocketbook Made from Burke's Skin," Surgeons' Hall Museums, Edinburgh, accessed March 16, 2022, https:// museum.rcsed.ac.uk/the-collection/key-collections/key -object-page/pocketbook-made-from-burkes-skin.

12 Ruiz, Cristina, "Executed Chinese Prisoners Likely Used in UK Exhibition," *The Art Newspaper*, January 25, 2021, https://

www.theartnewspaper.com/2021/01/25/executed-chinese
-prisoners-likely-used-in-uk-exhibition.

13 "Jeremy Bentham's Lifelong Plans for the Auto-Icon,"
University College London, March 4, 2021, https://www.ucl
.ac.uk/culture/news/jeremy-benthams-lifelong-plans-auto
-icon.

14 Bentham, Jeremy, *Auto-icon, or, Farther uses of the dead to the
living: a fragment from the mss of Jeremy Bentham* (London,
1842).

15 "Bentham's Life or Death Mask," University College London:
Bentham Project, May 17, 2018, https://www.ucl.ac.uk/
bentham-project/who-was-jeremy-bentham/representations/
old-radical/benthams-life-or-death-mask.

16 Quinn, Michael, "Writings on the Poor Laws, Volume II,"
University College London: Bentham Project, May 2007,
https://www.ucl.ac.uk/bentham-project/publications/works
-progress/writings-poor-laws-volume-ii.

17 "Report of the Committee on Anatomy," *The Lancet*
(London), September 6, 1828.

18 French, Roger, and Andrew Wear, *British Medicine in an Age
of Reform* (London: Routledge, 2015): 82.

19 Ridgway, Katherine, "Mortsafes," Virginia Department of
Historic Resources, April 30, 2021, https://www.dhr.virginia
.gov/cemetery-newsletter-content/mortsafes/.

20 "Beating London's Bodysnatchers," *Current Archaeology*,
September 20, 2017, https://archaeology.co.uk/articles/news/
beating-londons-bodysnatchers.htm.

21 "Coffin-Torpedo," Ohio History Central, accessed March 17,
2022, https://ohiohistorycentral.org/w/Coffin-Torpedo.

22 Onion, Rebecca, "The 'Cemetery Gun' Designed to Stop Grave Robbers," *Slate*, January 29, 2013, https://slate.com/human-interest/2013/01/cemetery-gun-invented-to-thwart-grave-robbers.html.

23 "African Burial Ground," New York Preservation Archive Project, https://www.nypap.org/preservation-history/african-burial-ground/.

24 Costa and Miller, "American Resurrection and the 1788 New York Doctors' Riot."

25 "Varieties," *Freedom's Journal* (New York, New York), March 30, 1827.

26 President's Commission on Slavery and the University, University of Virginia, 2018, https://slavery.virginia.edu/.

27 Davidson, James M., "'Resurrection Men' in Dallas: The Illegal Use of Black Bodies as Medical Cadavers (1900—1907)," *International Journal of Historical Archaeology* 11, no. 3 (2007): 193–220.

Chapter 5

1 "The Gower Cemetery," Edmond Historical Society, accessed March 17, 2022, https://www.edmondhistory.org/the-gower-cemetery/.

2 "African Americans in Early Edmond," Edmond Historical Society, accessed March 17, 2022, https://www.edmondhistory.org/blacks-in-early-edmond/.

3 Money, Jack, "Cemetery Gains Status," *The Oklahoman*, March 30, 1992, https://www.oklahoman.com/article/2389683/cemetery-gains-status.

4   Thomas, Myrtle Gower, 1993, interview by Mary Bond, *University of Central Oklahoma Oral History Project*.

5   O'Dell, Larry, "Senate Bill One," Oklahoma Historical Society: Encyclopedia of Oklahoma History and Culture, accessed March 18, 2022, https://www.okhistory.org/publications/enc/entry.php?entry=SE017.

6   Ogle, Abigail, "Volunteers Take down Fence Segregating Oklahoma Cemetery," KOCO, August 21, 2017, https://www.koco.com/article/volunteers-take-down-fence-segregating-oklahoma-cemetery/12041598.

7   "COVID-19 Initiative," The Hart Island Project, accessed March 18, 2022, https://www.hartisland.net/covid_initiative.

8   Sulzberger, A. G., "Gravestone from 1799 Is Found in Washington Square Park," *New York Times*, October 28, 2009, https://cityroom.blogs.nytimes.com/2009/10/28/gravestone-from-1799-is-found-in-washington-square-park/.

9   Geberer, Raanan, "Green-Wood Cemetery Reburies 200-Year-Old Bodies under Washington Square Park," *Brooklyn Daily Eagle*, March 2, 2021, https://brooklyneagle.com/articles/2021/03/02/historical-remains-found-during-construction-reburied-in-nyc/.

10 "Burials by prisoners," The Hart Island Project, accessed March 19, 2022, https://www.hartisland.net/history.

11 "Hart Island: Frequently Asked Questions," City of New York Department of Correction, accessed March 19, 2022, http://www.nyc.gov/html/doc/downloads/pdf/hart-island/FAQ-HartIsland040813.pdf.

12 "Hart Island: The City Cemetery," New York City Council, accessed March 19, 2022, https://council.nyc.gov/data/hart-island/.

13 Berger, Joseph, "City's Potter's Field in the Atomic Age," *New York Times*, July 31, 2009, https://www.nytimes.com/2009/08/02/nyregion/02bnukemb.html.

14 Brady, Emily, "A Chance to Be Mourned," *New York Times*, November 12, 2006, https://www.nytimes.com/2006/11/12/nyregion/thecity/12home.html.

15 Kilgannon, Corey, "Dead of AIDS and Forgotten in Potter's Field," *New York Times*, July 3, 2018, https://www.nytimes.com/2018/07/03/nyregion/hart-island-aids-new-york.html.

16 "AIDS Initiative," The Hart Island Project, accessed March 19, 2022, https://www.hartisland.net/aids_initiative.

17 "Undertakers Unit Warns of AIDS," *New York Times*, June 18, 1983.

18 Totenberg, Nina, and Domenico Montanaro, "Supreme Court Upholds Indiana Provision Mandating Fetal Burial or Cremation," *NPR*, May 28, 2019, https://www.npr.org/2019/05/28/727527860/supreme-court-upholds-indiana-provision-mandating-burial-or-cremation-of-fetal-r.

19 Ziegler, Heather, "Overdoses in W.Va. Drain Fund for Burials," *The Intelligencer*, March 5, 2017, https://www.theintelligencer.net/news/top-headlines/2017/03/overdoses-in-w-va-drain-fund-for-burials/.

20 Robinson, Lisa, "State Anatomy Board Overwhelmed with Unclaimed Bodies," WBAL, May 8, 2017, https://www.wbaltv.com/article/state-anatomy-board-overwhelmed-with-unclaimed-bodies/9622146.

21 Koranda, Jeannine, "State ends funds for funerals of poor," *The Wichita Eagle*, June 27, 2010, https://www.kansas.com/news/local/article1037434.html.

22 Lourgos, Angie Leventis, "Cook County's Social Worker for the Dead Helps the Unclaimed Find Final Resting Places," *The Chicago Tribune*, September 18, 2017, https://www.chicagotribune.com/news/ct-cook-county-medical-examiner-burials-met-20170917-story.html.

23 Kaplan, Jonah, "As Unclaimed Bodies Mount in North Carolina, Funeral Homes Urge Pre-Planning," ABC11 Raleigh-Durham, May 7, 2021, https://abc11.com/funeral-cost-virtual-unclaimed-bodies-service/10594256/.

24 "Remains of 37 People to Be Scattered in Puget Sound, If Left Unclaimed," KING 5 News, July 9, 2016, https://www.king5.com/article/news/local/remains-of-37-people-to-be-scattered-in-puget-sound-if-left-unclaimed/281-268530964.

25 Vega, Priscella, "Los Angeles County Virtually Mourns Its Unclaimed Dead," *Los Angeles Times*, December 1, 2021, https://www.latimes.com/california/story/2021-12-01/los-angeles-mourns-unclaimed-dead.

26 Allyn, Bobby, "In Philadelphia, Finding Dignity for Bodies Left Unclaimed," WHYY, May 25, 2016, https://whyy.org/segments/in-philadelphia-finding-dignity-for-bodies-left-unclaimed/.

27 Maryland Department of Health State Anatomy Board, "Annual Memorial Service," accessed March 19, 2022, https://health.maryland.gov/anatomy/Pages/Annual-Memorial-Service.aspx.

28 "Welcome to the Foundation for Dignity, Ltd.," The Foundation for Dignity, accessed March 19, 2022, https://www.thefoundationfordignity.org/.

29 Walsh, James D., "How Will New York City Respond to the Coronavirus?," *New York Magazine*, March 1, 2020,

https://nymag.com/intelligencer/2020/03/how-would-new
-york-city-respond-to-the-coronavirus.html.

30 Jackson, Lucas and Brendan McDermid, "New York City
Hires Laborers to Bury Dead in Hart Island Potter's Field
amid Coronavirus Surge," *Reuters*, April 9, 2020, https://www
.reuters.com/article/us-health-coronavirus-usa-hart-island
/new-york-city-hires-laborers-to-bury-dead-in-hart-island
-potters-field-amid-coronavirus-surge-idUSKCN21R398.

31 Columbia Journalism School's Stabile Center of Investigative
Journalism, "One in 10 Local COVID Victims Destined for
Hart Island, NYC's Potter's Field," *THE CITY*, March 24, 2021,
https://www.thecity.nyc/missing-them/2021/3/24/22349311/
nyc-covid-victims-destined-for-hart-island-potters-field.

32 "The Traveling Cloud Museum," The Hart Island Project,
accessed March 19, 2022, https://www.hartisland.net/.

Chapter 6

1 "The Space," Saint Peter's Church, accessed March 19, 2022,
https://www.saintpeters.org/the-space.

2 Alexander, Ron, "For AIDS Victims, a Church's Prayers - and
Food," *New York Times*, May 12, 1986, https://www.nytimes
.com/1986/05/12/style/for-aids-victims-a-church-s-prayers
-and-food.html.

3 Risser, David, "Funeral Workers Worry about AIDS Victims'
Bodies," *Daily Press*, July 27, 1989, https://www.dailypress
.com/news/dp-xpm-19890727-1989-07-27-8907270130-story
.html.

4   "Ashes Action," ACT UP Historical Archive, accessed March 19, 2022, https://actupny.org/reports/reportashes.html.

5   "Mungo Lady," National Museum of Australia, accessed March 19, 2022, https://www.nma.gov.au/defining-moments/resources/mungo-lady.

6   "Prelate Says Changing Times Lifted Catholic Cremation Ban," *New York Times*, June 8, 1964.

7   "One Who Fought for Italy; Joseph Mazzini's Bust Unveiled," *New York Times*, May 30, 1878.

8   Wilson, James Grant, "A Biographical Memoir of Bryant," *The Family Library of Poetry and Song, Memorial Edition* (New York: Fords, Howard, and Hulbert, 1880): 66.

9   Ibid., 67.

10 Sloam, Myrna, "Recalling the Bryant Legacy in Roslyn," accessed March 19, 2022, https://joomla.bryantlibrary.org/index.php?option=com_content&view=article&id=146:recalling-the-bryant-legacy-in-roslyn&catid=15&Itemid=181.

11 Gorini, Paolo, *Sulla purificazione dei morti per mezzo del fuoco: considerazioni, sperimenti e proposte* (Milan: Presso Natale Battezzati Editore, 1876): IX.

12 "Petrifaction," Collezione Anatomica "Paolo Gorini," accessed March 19, 2022, http://www.museogorini.com/pietrificazione_eng.php.

13 Gorini, Paolo, *Alla R. Accademia delle Scienze di Torino* (Italy: Tipografia C. Corradetti, 1864), 6.

14 "Paolo Gorini's Biography," Collezione Anatomica "Paolo Gorini," accessed March 19, 2022, http://www.museogorini.com/biografia_eng.php.

15 Gorini, Paolo, *Sulla purificazione dei morti per mezzo del fuoco*: 69.

16 "Cremation," Collezione Anatomica "Paolo Gorini," accessed March 19, 2022, http://www.museogorini.com/cremazione_eng.php.

17 Eassie, William, "Cremation In Its Bearings Upon Public Health," *The British Medical Journal* 2, no. 709 (1874): 134–38.

18 "The Eccentric Physician's Body Burned in His Own Furnace," *New York Times*, October 17, 1879.

19 Kilgore, Clay, "Looking Back: LeMoyne Crematory," *Observer-Reporter*, October 21, 2018, https://observer-reporter.com/news/looking_back/looking-back-lemoyne-crematory/article_5d7dbd30-d185-11e8-8bbd-e7e798921a72.html.

20 Roberts, Steven V., "Cremation Gaining Favor in U.S.," *New York Times*, December 6, 1970, https://www.nytimes.com/1970/12/06/archives/cremation-gaining-favor-in-us-cremation-is-gaining-favor-in-us.html.

21 Sanburn, Josh, "Cremation Is Now Outpacing Traditional Burial in the U.S.," *Time*, August 2016, https://time.com/4425172/cremation-outpaces-burial-u-s/.

22 2021 Annual Statistics Report, Cremation Association of North America, https://www.cremationassociation.org/page/IndustryStatistics.

23 Miner, Casey, "Oakland's Chapel of the Chimes: For the Dead, and the Living," KQED, July 5, 2014, https://www.kqed.org/news/141156/hidden-gem-oaklands-chapel-of-the-chimes-columbarium-is-place-for-living-and-dead.

24 Salvarezza, Michael, and Christopher P. Weaver, "Florida's Neptune Memorial Reef: A Dive Site for Underwater Taphophiles," *California Diver*, February 23, 2022, https://californiadiver.com/floridas-neptune-memorial-reef-a-dive-site-for-underwater-taphophiles-223/.

25 "Roddenberry Gets His Flight," *Newsweek*, May 8, 1994, https://www.newsweek.com/roddenberry-gets-his-flight-188706.

26 Fletcher, Chris, "'Burying' a Man on the Moon," NBC News, December 1, 2005, https://www.nbcnews.com/id/wbna3077929.

27 Mullen, Jethro, "NASA Probe Passes Pluto, Carrying Ashes of Man Who Discovered It," *CNN*, July 13, 2015, https://www.cnn.com/2015/07/13/us/nasa-pluto-new-horizons-clyde-tombaugh-ashes/index.html.

28 "Global Mercury Assessment 2018," UN Environment Programme, March 4, 2019, https://www.unep.org/resources/publication/global-mercury-assessment-2018.

29 "Crematorium Tried to Use Bodies to Heat Houses," *The Local Norway*, March 25, 2015, https://www.thelocal.no/20150325/oslo-crematorium/.

Chapter 7

1 Connors, Thomas G., "The Romantic Landscape: Washington Irving, Sleepy Hollow, and the Rural Cemetery Movement," in *Mortal Remains: Death in Early America* ed. by Nancy Isenberg and Andrew Burstein (Philadelphia: University of Pennsylvania Press, 2012): 187-204.

2 "Reminiscences of the late Washington Irving," *The Knickerbocker,* Volume 55 (United States: Peabody, 1860).

3 "Green Burial," Sleepy Hollow Cemetery, accessed March 20, 2022, https://sleepyhollowcemetery.org/green-burial/.

4 "GBC-Certified Cemeteries in the United States and Canada," Green Burial Council, accessed March 20, 2022, https://www.greenburialcouncil.org/cemeteries.html.

5 "Cemetery," Town of Rhinebeck, NY, accessed March 20, 2022, https://www.rhinebeckny.gov/cemetery.html.

6 Johanson, Mark, "Surprise! The World's Oldest Mummies Are Not in Egypt," *CNN*, May 1, 2019, https://www.cnn.com/travel/article/worlds-oldest-mummies-chile/index.html.

7 Lyons, Elizabeth, "Chinese Jades," *Expedition* magazine of the Penn Museum, 1978.

8 Moynihan, Colin, "A Quest to Recognize Forgotten Achievements Still Relevant in Everyday Life," *New York Times*, May 27, 2014, https://www.nytimes.com/2014/05/27/nyregion/recognizing-bits-of-our-forgotten-history.html.

9 Carol, Anne, "Embalming and materiality of death (France, nineteenth century)," *Mortality*, Taylor & Francis (Routledge), 2019, 24 (2): 183-192.

10 Laderman, Gary, *The Sacred Remains: American Attitudes toward Death, 1799-1883* (New Haven: Yale University Press, 1996): 116.

11 "Obsequies of Col. Ellsworth," *New York Times*, May 27, 1861.

12 Fitzharris, Lindsey, "Embalming and the Civil War," National Museum of Civil War Medicine, February 20, 2016, https://www.civilwarmed.org/embalming1.

13 Holmes, Oliver Wendell, "My Hunt after the Captain," *The Atlantic Monthly*, December 1862.

14 "Photography at Antietam," Antietam National Battlefield (U.S. National Park Service), accessed March 20, 2022, https://www.nps.gov/anti/learn/historyculture/photography.htm.

15 Gardner, Alexander, "A Harvest of Death," *Photographic Sketch Book of the War* (1866).

16 Bumiller, Elisabeth, "U.S. Lifts Photo Ban on Military Coffins," *New York Times*, December 7, 2009, https://www.nytimes.com/2009/02/27/world/americas/27iht-photos.1.20479953.html.

17 "History of Formaldehyde," Formacare, European Chemical Industry Council, https://www.formacare.eu/about-formaldehyde/history-of-formaldehyde/.

18 *Memorial Record of the Nation's Tribute to Abraham Lincoln,* compiled by B. F. Morris (Washington, DC: W.H. & O.H. Morrison, 1865): 41.

19 "The Lincoln Funeral Train," Illinois History & Lincoln Collections, August 30, 2019, https://publish.illinois.edu/ihlc-blog/2019/08/30/the-lincoln-funeral-train/.

20 "The Body of Mr. Lincoln in New York," *Philadelphia North American and United States Gazette*, April 25, 1865.

21 Tebb, William, and Edward Perry Vollum, *Premature Burial and How It May Be Prevented: With Special Reference To Trance, Catalepsy And Other Forms Of Suspended Animation* (London : Swan Sonnenschein & Co., 1896): 229.

22 Poe, Edgar Allan, "The Premature Burial," *The Philadelphia Dollar Newspaper*, 1844.

23 "Buried Alive: A Terrible Thing to Contemplate," *The Sentinel* (Carlisle, Pennsylvania), June 23, 1844.

24 Leonetti, G., et al., "Evidence of pin implantation as a means of verifying death during the Great Plague of Marseilles (1722)," *Journal of Forensic Sciences*, 42(4) (1997): 744–748.

25 Sanders, Laura, "New Guidance on Brain Death Could Ease Debate over When Life Ends," *Science News*, August 10, 2020, https://www.sciencenews.org/article/new-guidance-brain -death-debate-over-when-life-ends.

26 Ubaid, Mir, "New York's Muslims Struggle to Bury Their Dead," *Al Jazeera*, March 7, 2016, https://www.aljazeera.com /features/2016/3/7/what-is-a-muslim-funeral-like-in-new -york.

27 Cross, Pam, "Walpole cemetery plans have environmental, religious group at odds," WCVB-TV, May 8, 2015, https:// www.wcvb.com/article/walpole-cemetery-plans-have -environmental-religious-group-at-odds/8222182.

28 "Lawsuit against Stafford Co. Dropped after Muslim Cemetery in Virginia Approved," *Associated Press*, October 14, 2021, https://wtop.com/stafford-county/2021/10/lawsuit -against-stafford-co-dropped-after-muslim-cemetery-in -virginia-approved/.

29 Veigel, Wyndi, "Muslim Cemetery: Residents Want It Dead," *Farmersville Times*, July 9, 2015, https://farmersvilletimes.com /2015/07/09/muslim-cemetery-residents-want-it-dead/.

30 Abrams, Abigail, "New England Town Rejects a Muslim Cemetery. Now the Feds Are Investigating a Civil Rights Violation," *Time*, August 18, 2016, https://time.com/4457682/ muslim-cemetery-rejected-feds-investigate.

31 Boeri, David, "Islamic Society Wins Permit for Muslim Cemetery in Dudley after Protracted, Bitter Clash," WBUR, March 3, 2017, https://www.wbur.org/news/2017/03/03/ dudley-muslim-cemetery-permit.

32 "One More Opportunity Knocks at Your Door," *Oklahoma City Times* (Oklahoma City, Okla.), November 9, 1916.

33 De Simone, Amy, "The Glass Coffin," Corning Museum of Glass, October 25, 2012, https://blog.cmog.org/2012/10/25/the-glass-coffin/.

34 Fisk, Almond, "Review of Improvement in Coffins," United States Patent Office, issued November 14, 1848.

35 "The Woman in the Iron Coffin," PBS, October 3, 2018.

36 Slocum, Josh, "What You Should Know about Exploding Caskets," *Washington Post*, August 11, 2014, https://www.washingtonpost.com/posteverything/wp/2014/08/11/what-you-should-know-about-exploding-caskets/.

37 Dao, James, "Last Inspection: Precise Ritual of Dressing Nation's War Dead," *New York Times,* May 25, 2013, https://www.nytimes.com/2013/05/26/us/intricate-rituals-for-fallen-americans-troops.html.

38 Meyers, Maureen S., David Breetzke, and Henry Holt, "Arsenic and Old Graves," *Advances in Archaeological Practice* 9 (1), December 22, 2020: 34–40.

Chapter 8

1 Phillips, Rosalie S., "A Burial Place for the Jewish Nation Forever," *Publications of the American Jewish Historical Society*, no. 18 (1909): 93–122.

2 Hassan, Adeel, "Ashes to Ashes. Dust to Dust. Or, in Washington State, You Could Now Be Compost," *New York Times*, May 22, 2019, https://www.nytimes.com/2019/05/22/us/human-composting-washington.html.

3 "Our Model," Recompose, accessed March 21, 2022, https://recompose.life/our-model/.

4   Hindi, Saja, "Colorado Becomes Only 2nd State in the U.S.
To Allow Composting of Human Bodies," *Denver Post*, May
10, 2021, https://www.denverpost.com/2021/05/10/human
-composting-colorado-law-death/.

5   Lee, Webster, "To Lie Down in Green Pastures: How the
Catholic Church is leading the way in green burial," Green
Burial Council, accessed March 21, 2022, https://www
.greenburialcouncil.org/the-catholic-church-and-green-burial
.html.

6   "Composting of Human Bodies: Memorandum of
Opposition," New York State Catholic Conference, January
7, 2022, https://www.nyscatholic.org/composting-of-human
-bodies/.

7   Carrns, Ann, "Funeral Homes Slow to Put Prices Online,"
New York Times, February 2, 2018, https://www.nytimes.com
/2018/02/02/your-money/funeral-homes-prices.html.

8   Slocum, Joshua, and Stephen Brobeck for Funeral Consumers
Alliance and Consumer Federation of America, "A Needle
in a Haystack-Finding Funeral Prices Online in 26 State
Capitals," January 29, 2018, https://funerals.org/wp-content
/uploads/2018/01/1-29-18-Funeral-Report-Online-Web
-Pricing-Disclosure-Report.pdf.

9   "2021 NFDA General Price List Study Shows Funeral Costs
Not Rising as Fast as Rate of Inflation," National Funeral
Directors Association, https://nfda.org/news/media-center
/nfda-news-releases/id/6182/2021-nfda-general-price-list
-study-shows-funeral-costs-not-rising-as-fast-as-rate-of
-inflation.

10 Waters, Michael, "Cremation Borrows a Page from
the Direct-To-Consumer Playbook," *New York Times*,

February 3, 2022, https://www.nytimes.com/2022/02/03/business/cremation-startups-direct-to-consumer.html.

11 The World Wide Cemetery, accessed March 21, 2022, https://cemetery.org/our-story/.

12 "Michael Kibbee 1964-1997," The World Wide Cemetery, accessed March 21, 2022, https://cemetery.org/michael-kibbee/.

13 Elliott, Josh K., "'Final Fantasy' Gamers Hold Online Funeral for Player Who Died of COVID-19," *Global News*, April 17, 2020, https://globalnews.ca/news/6832247/coronavirus-video-game-funeral/.

14 Harper, E., "Robin Williams Tribute Arrives in Warlords of Draenor," *Engadget*, September 4, 2014, https://www.engadget.com/2014-09-04-robin-williams-tribute-arrives-in-warlords-of-draenor.html.

15 "Marvin 'Popcorn' Sutton (1946-2009)," Find a Grave, accessed March 21, 2022, https://www.findagrave.com/memorial/220369882/marvin-sutton.

16 Newton, Casey, "When Her Best Friend Died, She Used Artificial Intelligence to Keep Talking to Him," *The Verge*, October 6, 2016, https://www.theverge.com/a/luka-artificial-intelligence-memorial-roman-mazurenko-bot.

17 Harmon, Amy, "Making Friends with a Robot Named Bina48," *New York Times*, July 4, 2010, https://www.nytimes.com/2010/07/05/science/05robotside.html.

18 Sample, Ian, "Firm Plans Human DNA Tree Memorial," *The Guardian*, April 30, 2004, https://www.theguardian.com/science/2004/apr/30/genetics.highereducation.

19 "Researchers Reimagine the Future Cemetery at Arnos Vale," University of Bath's Centre for Death & Society,

March, 1 2016, https://www.bath.ac.uk/announcements
/researchers-reimagine-the-future-cemetery-at-arnos
-vale/.

20 "WPA 2.0," Columbia GSAPP DeathLAB, accessed March 21,
2022, http://deathlab.org/wpa-2-0/.

21 "Desmond Tutu: Body of South African Hero to Be
Aquamated," *BBC News*, December 31, 2021, https://www.bbc
.co.uk/news/world-africa-59842728.

22 Sini, Rozina, "Would You Get Buried in a Mushroom Suit like
Luke Perry?," *BBC News*, May 6, 2019, https://www.bbc.com/
news/48140812.

Chapter 9

1 "About the Woodlands," The Woodlands, accessed March 22,
2022, https://www.woodlandsphila.org/about.

2 *The Stranger's Guide in Philadelphia* (Philadelphia: Lindsay &
Blakiston, 1861): 232.

3 "Rethinking Urban Grasslands," Green-Wood Cemetery,
accessed March 22, 2022, https://www.green-wood.com/
rethinking-urban-grasslands/.

4 Crosby, Betsy, "The Resurrection of Congressional Cemetery,"
National Trust for Historic Preservation, January 1, 2012,
https://savingplaces.org/stories/congressional-cemetery
-resurrection.

5 "The Bridge to Crafts Careers Program," World Monuments
Fund, accessed March 22, 2022, https://www.wmf.org/project/
bridge-crafts-careers-program.

6   "FAQs," Oakland Cemetery, accessed March 22, 2022, https://oaklandcemetery.com/faqs/.

7   "Invisible Flock," website of Dorothy O'Connor, accessed March 22, 2022, https://www.dorothyoconnor.com/Public-Art-Projects/The-Invisible-Flock/.

8   Bentley, Rosalind, "'Praise House' at Oakland Cemetery to Celebrate Juneteenth," *Atlanta Journal-Constitution*, June 16, 2021, https://www.ajc.com/life/praise-house-at-oakland-cemetery-to-celebrate-juneteenth/VRQT2DHZ2NDEVIE UILPZNZUFFY/.

9   "Memorial To A Marriage," website of Patricia Cronin, accessed March 22, 2022, https://www.patriciacronin.net/memorial.html.

10 Bauld, Laura, "The Power of Patricia Cronin's 'Memorial to a Marriage,'" *Art UK*, February 1, 2021, https://artuk.org/discover/stories/the-power-of-patricia-cronins-memorial-to-a-marriage.

INDEX